Our Ancestors Through The Ages

Our Ancestors Through *The Ages*

EVELYN HAYWOOD FRIEND

Library of Congress Control Number: 2013911598

ISBN 978-1-953048-09-7 (sc)

Printed in the United States of America.
To order additional copies of this book, contact:

Writers Branding
1800-608-6550
www.writersbranding.com
orders@writersbranding.com

TABLE OF CONTENTS

OUR ANCESTORS THROUGH THE AGES

SINCE MOST GOOD SPEECHES START with a joke, why not start this book with one which was found on the Internet.

From Creation to Evolution

A little girl asked her mother, “How did the human race begin”? Her mother said, “Many years ago God made Adam and Eve and they had children and that is how all mankind was made”. A few days later the little girl asked her father the same question. Her father said “Many years ago there were monkeys and a branch of the family evolved into the human race”. The confused girl returned to her mother and said “Mother, how is it possible that you told me that the human race was created by God and papa said they developed from monkeys”? The mother said, “Well dear, I told you about my side of the family and your father told you about his side of the family”.

THE PURPOSE OF THIS BOOK

THE PURPOSE OF THIS BOOK is to document the lives of Frederick William HAYWOOD and Mary Minnie Gurney, and their ancestors and their descendants. The material was collected and provided by their descendants, brothers, Sisters, aunts, uncles, cousins and children. In the interest of all the families as well as future generation.

ACKNOWLEDGEMENTS

WE WISH TO THANK ALL family members who dug into their records, as well as their memories to contribute to this publication. Many contacted other family members, as well.

One comes to mind is Joyce Allen. She is the wife of Charlie Allen, their home is in England. When she would go on trips to Ireland and Scotland she would talk with family plus get info from churches and other places were info was kept. Without her a lot of this would not be possible. Thank you Joyce. Also Nancy Gurney (Hulley) Sandra Gurney (Squire) and Billy Allen. Also big thanks to all of you to Dave Simpson my son and his wife Heidi and their daughter Rylli for their input in sharing their thoughts in how to put it together. Also my husband Bill who help with how to set up things, and my daughter Rose-Anna for getting a publisher. Edward Scea for helping with the trees. The librarians, cemetery custodians, land records offices etc, who made their records available for our research. And to me for getting it done so we can enjoy it and learn about our ancestors. You all can add in the future ones and sure them with everyone. To everyone a big Thank-You.

DISCLAIMERS

GREAT EFFORT HAS BEEN MADE to ensure that correct data is reported,

However, no doubt there will be errors. When possible, reports were sent to family members for review from time to time.

Errors were detected, this happens when there is not enough information or they received the wrong information. Since not everyone has had an opportunity to review their own data errors are very possible.

OUR SEARCH BEGINS

SEARCHING FOR ANCESTORS IS NOT a straight forward project, and a lot of time and research has been put into it, from a lot of people sharing their information. As I go through the families I will be adding more names. We will begin with the Haywood's and the Gurney's. We hope that one of the Haywood's or the Gurney's you found are part of your family. We found many families, with similar names but can't be 100 per cent they are related to your families. But with research we can come close. One way is from birth, death, and marriage certificate.

ANCESTORS

If you could see your ancestors
All standing in a row
Now turn the question right about
Would you be proud of them
And take another view.
Or don't you really know?
When you shall meet your ancestors
Will they be proud of you?
Stange Discoveries are often made,

In climbing the family tree,
Sometimes one is found in line
Who shocks the progeny?
If you could see your ancestors
All standing in a row,
Perhaps there might be one or two
You wouldn't care to know.

—Author Unknown.

THE LONG ROUGH JOURNEY FROM OLD TO NEW

THE JOURNEY FROM OLD TO new, from the shores of Britain England, Ireland, and Scotland, to the shores of Canada. They sailed across the Atlantic in sailing vessels, which were often packed beyond endurance by greedy masters.

It was very busy for passengers immigrating to Canada in particular Quebec, which gave the shipbuilders access to Canadian lumber. This was carried in the same boat on return journeys. At Quebec the travelers transferred to a river-steamer and proceeded to Montreal. Or other places in Quebec if that was their destination. My grandparents and their children stead in Sorel Quebec, at that time. My mother Mary Minnie Gurney came to Canada from North Londonderry Ireland a place called Derry, when she was 19 years old, by boat in 1924 the name of the boat was the Duchess Of Bedford to Quebec then she came to Toronto Ontario Canada; she had been sponsored by a family name Wile's. She had to work for them for five years to work off her passage. She came five years before my uncle Lewis Gurney came by boat from North Londonderry Ireland Derry to Quebec city on the Montroyal(ex-EMPRESS OF BRITAIN on AUGUST 2, 1929. He went to a farm where he worked off his passage. From here west, one could, by paying prohibitive fares, reach Lake Ontario by alternate shifts of stagecoach and steamer, but by far the greater number travelled by bateau or by Durham boat. The bateau was a large, flat bottomed skiff, thirty to forty feet long, eight to ten wide, and built sharp at both ends. It was propelled by oars and sail. Progress was necessarily slow. It took a whole week to go from Montreal to Prescott. Sometimes as many as one hundred persons would be crowed together in a single thirty foot bateau, scorched by sun or drenched by rain, as their rude craft crept reluctantly up the river. At last, at Prescott or Kingston, transfer was made to a lake steamer, which carried the pioneers on the lake port nearest their destination.

There were two general routes from the lake front to the inland townships. Those who went to Emily or Ops went north from Cobourg or Port hope. One trail lay north-northwest through Cavan(the modern Millbrook), another went north to Peterborough and then northwest towards Emily, still another cut across from Peterborough to Chemong Lake, whence access to the remoter township could be had by canoe. This is just a little history of how people got around back then. To-day thing are a lot difference Travel is a lot easier with all the different ways one can go. Like Bus, Plain, Train or Car.

DOWN MEMORY LANE

What we found

THE INFORMATION WE HAVE ON my father, Frederick William Haywood was that his mother Annie Roberts and his father Frederick William Haywood, came from Liverpool Lancashire England. He came from a family of five children and he was born in 1876, and his wife Annie Roberts was born in 1879, she came from a family of four children. They came to Canada with two children, Richard Haywood born 1907 and Doris Haywood born1910. When they came to Canada it was to a place called Sorel Quebec Canada. That is where a son was born, Frederick William Haywood on December 16th 1907. A few years later they moved to Toronto Ontario Canada. The first section of this book is about Liverpool Lancashire England, and Londonderry North Ireland. And a little about each person, also data reports for Fred and Mary's ancestors. This is far from complete, but it is what has been collected to this point in time. The second section is about Frederick William Haywood and his family after they came to Canada, with their children, and their brothers and sisters and so on down the line. The next part is about the Gurney's, William Gurney and his wife Sarah Wallace and their children, which were seven. And brothers and sisters and so on down the line. Within each child's section is a summary of the data for their children and descendants. Some families choose not to provide data for all members of their line, or didn't have it.

We will do the best we can with what we have, and hope.

You will be pleased with what you see and read.

THE TOWN OF WESTON IN TORONTO CANADA

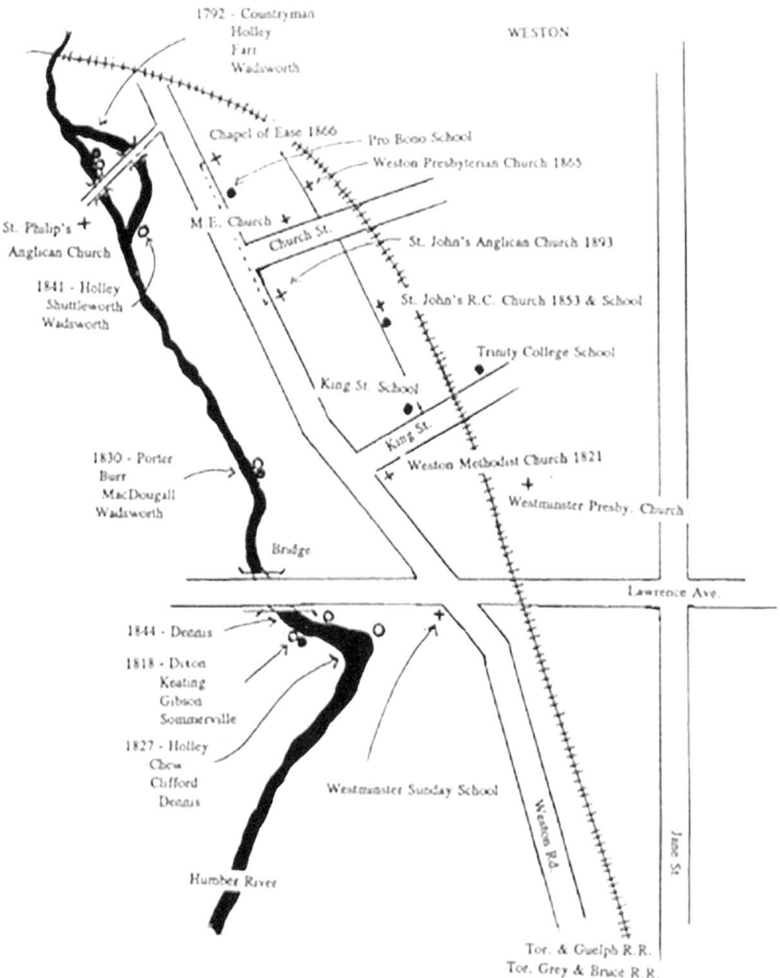

Weston first was a Village becomes a separate legal village incorporating in 1881 and continuing to grow until 1915 when it became a town. It was still growing and developing in 1954, when Metropolitan Toronto was formed, and Weston was attached back as part of the Township of York.

Weston Town Hall was completed in 1885, on the northwest corner of Weston Rd. and Little Ave.

The name Weston was given by Charles and William Wadsworth, to their land around the mill and store on the west bank of the Humber. The brothers had been born in or near Weston-super-Mare, Somerset, England. When Charles Wadsworth bought the store and flour mill, in 1828, from John and James Farr, they wanted to change the previous owner's name of Farr's Mills. Prior to the Farr's occupancy, the area was just known as, "The Humber". The name "Farr's Mill" was difficult to drop, since it had been in use by farmers and the Quarter Sessions for at least ten years. It was probably after the establishing of a Post office, in 1841, that the name Weston became official and in general use. The settlement first developed on a three acre, narrow strip, on the west bank valley of the Humber River, on Lot # 22 close to the present St. Phillip's Road. The main street of the settlement was Weston Road. By 1810 it was a regular wagon trail to the mills from Dundas Street and, in 1841 it was planked by the Weston Plank Road Company. The street toll-gates were supposed to raise enough money to replace any worn plants. The community then grew up on either side of Weston Road. In on the east by the railway built in 1856. Meanwhile, in spite of all the bustle of building homes and mills and getting resettled on the east bank, worship services for the adults and education for the children become a strong concern.

ın's Chapel as it was called in 1856 when it was ıed by the Rev. Wm. A. Johnson and erected on ry Road. In 1893, it was moved to its present site on Street just south of Church Street.

St. John's Anglican Church in its present location on Main Street just south of Church Street. From 1856 to 1893 it was located on Rectory Road and served as the chapel for Trinity College Boys' School.

In an English settlement, where the religion was the Church of England, and perfectly natural for the settlers to want Anglican religious services. I myself was raised up in the St John's Anglican church in Weston. These were held in homes until Edward and Thomas Masson [distillers] donated land on the west bank for a church. It was built of frame construction in 1828 and was known as St. Phillips. A fire in May 1888 destroyed the frame church but a beautiful brick gothic style new one was built in 1894. It continued to grow and prosper with additions in 1936 and 1957. Over a few years there were defiance kinds of churches. Weston Town Hall was completed in 1885, on the northwest corner of Weston RD. Little Ave. King St. school was built in 1892, on King St. just cast of Weston Rd. Captain John Pirritte, a former teacher in the army garrisons at Halifax and Kingston. Was anxious to start a school for he and his wife had several small children of their own. And did so in their own small clapboard home. The attendance soon forced firstly a change to a larger house across the road in 1842.

In that time there was a change of teachers, to Major John Paul. By 1849 the council of the Home District had taken over the school and acquired the site for a larger frame school. However, the rapid growth of the 50's again forced the need for a still larger school building. At this time a modern brick building on the east side of Weston Road was erected in 1860. This pro bono school served the community well for the next thirty years until 1892, when a new larger school was built on King Street. The "pro bono" school became the Long staff Pump factory. The new King Street School acquired a school bell, which gradually become the village bell, and not only called the children to school for nine o'clock, but summoned the men to work at seven in the morning. It also served as a fire alarm and nine o'clock curfew. The village soon became accustomed to the pleasant gonging of the school bell. By 1912, more space was needed. After temporary space was utilized in local churches and the Town Hall, four additional rooms were added to the King Street School. Eventually, it was renamed H. J. Alexander School. As the village spread across the tracts to the east, a school was a definite requirement for this area. So in 1919 in spite of a "no" vote by the ratepayers, the Board built Memorial School. It was obvious that secondary education should be available "at home, in town" By the mid 1850's once the fumbling over the name of the settlement was decided and the decision to use the east bank was confirmed, a mere 500 audacious souls suggested they started a grammar school. The necessary charter for a "grammar "school was obtained and in 1857 classes, started with only twenty boys in the Methodist Church and then, across the road on King Street {corner of Main Street} in the stone house of the Porter family. The following year a brick building was erected one quarter of one mile farther along on King Street. This was the first grammar school {High School} to be built without municipal or government money. The first principal, until 1865 was Rev. John B. Logan, M.A., from Scotland, followed by James Hodgson, until 1871, when the school name was changed to Weston High School and John Somerville took over. After a fire in 1874, and a rebuilding immediately, the school served the community until 1913, when a new High School was built on William Street. As mentioned under churches Roman Catholic students, in Weston received their own separate school organized in 1856. In another school was built in 1921 with the continued growth. Another school that developed in Weston in the 1860's was the school for boys, under Dr. Johnson of St. Philip's. It was officially opened, in 1865, as Trinity College School with an affiliation to Trinity University. The school soon out grew the old tavern, near the church, in which they had King Street, at Rosemont. However, its sojourn in Weston was short lived, in that, by 1871, due to both financial and emotional difficulties, it was moved to Port Hope. Also a fifth school that had a short continuance in Weston was “The Banks Private School”. This was operated as early as 1850 by Dr. John H. Banks and his wife, in their home on Main Street. Nevertheless in 1871 this school too had closed and students now no choice but the “pro bono” school. The first registered plan of Weston was dated July 1846. It was prepared by John Stoughton Dennis, son of John Dennis of Mount Dennis fame. Since this was before the disastrous flood of 1850, the settlement was mainly on the western bank. The decision to move to the York side, of course, started to fill in along the Weston Plank Road. Previously, the hamlet was squeezed onto a narrow three acre strip and now in the beginning, it was compressed between the Humber River on the west, and the two railway lines on the east. Someone commented that Weston yards wide. Nevertheless, the settlement grew quite quickly after 1850; so that, within twenty years, the population had doubled to almost one thousand souls was a village three miles long, but only a few hundred.

The Weston Police Department started in the early 1880’s with only one constable to watch over the village. The constable’s duties were to be vigilant and active at all times to enforce the observance of the By-Laws of the Municipality. On the occasion that someone was found breaking the law the Constable had the authority to detain the offender for up to ten days in the village lock-up, located in the basement of the Town Hall.

In addition to his law enforcement duties, the Village Constable was also Village Sanitary Inspector and Truant Officer. He had to inspect regularly all streets, lanes, sidewalks, crossing and culverts, reporting on their condition to the council and supervising repairs. Culverts and watercourses needed special attention as it was the Constable’s job to prevent, If at all possible from remaining on streets and sidewalks. Snow in the winter and dust and dirt in the summer had to be cleaned from the streets crossings and sidewalks in front of vacant lots.

Of course the appearance of the lawn at the Town Hall had to be well kept. There the Constable, as the Town Hall caretaker, cut the grass and weeded regularly. He also carried the keys and had to be on hand to open the Hall for meetings held there. Inside he keeps the room “clean, scrubbed and dusted”, Particularly the Council Chamber. Any man wanting the job of Constable had to be prepared for a good share of exercise. He was to make his inspection rounds, check on the Hotels, pass along Main Street at least once each evening and ring the bell on the Town Hall, as well as the school bell four times daily. He attended all public gatherings to maintain decorum and made a report regularly at all Council meeting.

Over the years law enforcement priorities' changed from keeping cows off the sidewalks to regulation of increasing, demanding traffic. The jobs of Sanitary Inspector and Truant Officer were taken over by others, leaving the Constable free to focus his attention on matters concerning the law. By 1954 the force had expanded to include fourteen members. These included a Chief Constable, four Patrol Sergeants, seven First Class Constables, and two Second class Constables.

As of December 31, 1957, all Police Officers, School Crossing Guards, and Temporary Constables were no longer employed by Weston, when the Weston Police Force was amalgamated with the Metropolitan Toronto Police force. Weston was fortunate in having this force for the routine duties that the men performed as well as for the acts of bravery and benevolence shown at times of emergency such as that of Hurricane Hazel in 1954.

Interior of Lawrence's Grocery Store. *L. to R.:* Fred Simpson, Con McEwen and Bill Lawrence (owner).

David Holly was very active in Weston area, with buying or leasing lots on either bank of the Humber. By 1819, Joseph, his son, had erected a mill, distillery, and a store. The mill complex was on lot #22.

This consisted of a flour mill with two run of stone, a saw mill, distillery and a store.

Street cars on the Toronto Suburban Railway through Weston (circa 1900).

By the 1800's, "railway fever" was in the air. It started in 1849, with the passing of The Railway Act, which guaranteed part of the cost. By 1853 over fifty charters for railways were issued and that same year, in Canada West, the first train left Toronto for Mach ell's Corners [Aurora]. To be a station on the railway line was a terrific growth factor to the Town of Weston. The first railway to come through Weston was the Ontario, Simcoe and Huron Railway built through the town in 1853. It helped considerably to increase the efficiency of the mail service previously handled by the stage coaches. Farmers found it ideal for transportation of produce and supplies to and from Toronto. The Ontario, Simcoe and Huron Railway was commonly called the "Oats, Straw and Hay" Railway. It later changed its name to the Northern Railway of Canada. A few years later Weston was considered as a station for the new Grand Trunk Railway. Weston citizens were eager to have the railway come through the town. However difficulties arose and a rivalry started up when Mr. John Scarlett made an offer to the railway company in an effort to persuade them to build through on the west bank of the Humber. For a while it looked bad for the town but Weston finally won out.

On July 1, 1856 celebrations in Weston heralded the opening of the Grand Trunk line through Weston. The Grand Trunk Railway soon became the most important railway system in eastern Canada and remained so for many years.

In 1870 a group of Toronto merchants planned to put into action the idea of a narrow gauge tract of 3'6". Up until that time a standard gauge of 5'6" was used. The Grand Trunk allowed the group's company, The Toronto Grey and Bruce Railway Co. to put in an extra rail along the Grand Trunk right of way.

Above: Grand Trunk Railway Station (later C.N.R.) showing *L to R:* Tot Wynn, Mrs. Watson and child, Ewart Raymond, Dorothy Charlton, Art Hill, Mrs. Fred "Jenny" Hill, Norma Charlton, Mr. Fred Hill (station agent), George Holley.

Opposite: Turning of the sod by H.R.H. Prince Arthur of Connaught (later Governor General of Canada), at the north end of Weston, for the extension of the Toronto Grey & Bruce Railway (later C.P.R.), October 5, 1869.

On Tuesday, October the fifth 1869, Weston was honored with the presence of royalty. Prince Arthur of Connaught, later Duke of Connaught, and war-time Governor-General of Canada performed the turning of the first sod of the Toronto, Grey and Bruce Railway. The ceremony took place beside the tracks at Oct St. Virtually all of Weston and many of Toronto's elite turned out to witness the ceremony and join in the celebrations afterwards. Despite such auspicious beginnings, the Toronto Grey and Bruce Railway ran into difficulties because of the size of the gauge. Between 1881 and 1883, they had the gauge changed from 3'6" to the prevailing measure of 4' 8 ½". In 1884 the Toronto Grey and Bruce Railway was leased to the Canadian Pacific Railway.

The coming of the First World War affected the railways severely. By 1917 both the Grand Trunk and the Canadian Northern were bankrupt. In the midst of a war, the government found itself helping both railways financially. Thus, due to amalgamation, the two railways running through Weston today are publically owned through the Canadian National and the Canadian Pacific Railways. Because of improved roadways and the coming of the automobile, Weston does not rely on the railways as it once did. However, Weston cannot easily forget the prosperity brought with the coming of the iron rails.

Fire Fighting In Weston

Weston did not have an official fire department until the end of Second World War, when Ernest Mc Guinnis was voted in to the position of first fire department chief. He was very popular with his mates and was qualified for the position became of his fire fighting experiences in London during the war.

Before 1854 Weston relied on kindhearted neighbors to bail them out if there was a fire. In 1912 a volunteers service was formed and meetings were held on the first Thursday of every month, excluding the summer months of July and August. At first the volunteers relied on only the neighbor's calls. Later the Moffat Stove Co. started using their bell to warn the people. The Fire Department was well respected in the town, and held great weight in public opinion. There were four stationed hand reels in the town and at the sound of the fire bell there was a mad dash to the reel closest to the fire.

The first fire hall was located in the Activity Centre on Little Ave. Behind it was a tall tower where they hung up their hoses to-day. Weston had four fire trucks throughout its history. The first one was a soused up Baby Grand Chevy which was bought in 1932 but the car was really made in 1929. It was first put to use in May 1932 for a fire in the Cruikshank building. The second truck was a General Motor Corp, vehicle purchased in 1942. The third was bought in 1962 and the last one was purchased just before amalgamation with York Borough.

When Mr. McGuinnis was the fire chief he still worked with volunteers. As the years went on, businessmen refused to leave their customers and shops to fight fires. Finally Weston and York Township amalgamated and the men were separated to station all over York, with

Mr. Mc Guinnis becoming District Chief. In that year, 1967, Weston's Fire Department had its final tribute at the Beverly Hills to every person ever associated with them. This is a little history of the town I grow up in the 1936 and back when it was formed, a part of its history is in Toronto, Ontario, Canada. To-day it has changed but still has it's things like the library and St John's Anglican church.

By the Weston Historical Society

Weston Centennial Song 1881- to May 31, 1981
[Words and music by Eleanor Edwards]

Oh we've been proud of Weston.
For a hundred years and more.
From a Countryman's first saw-mill.
To the sound of the City's roar.

From the first Church, a log cabin.
To the mighty spires we see.
Our historic homes still standing
In proud for thee.

There are many who have loved you.
They were early pioneers.
For the streets now bear the proud names.
Of those long gone from here.

You have weathered well, dear Weston.
From floods and fires you've survived.
From Wars and demolition.
To a Centennial you've arrived

I hope that many who read this will recall their own association with all the changes that occur during the years and ahead when children and grandchildren live in this same town.

The End.

THE FAMILIES OF THE HAYWOODS & GURNEYS AND THEIR DESCENDANTS WITH THEIR STORIES

THE FAMILIES OF THE HAYWOOD'S AND GURNEYS AND THEIR DESCENDANTS BEFORE THE STORIES

The Introduction

Our Ancestors are from England, Ireland, Scotland, U.S.A. and Canada.

Sum have traveled to Canada and the U.S.A. Others have stated were they were born. But where ever they maybe we always keep in contacted, as much as possible and love them for they are our family. And it is nice to go back into each line to find out about other those passed on. Finding your roots is important. It's a way to become closer and to find out a little about them, were they were born, what they did for a living, how many in the family and how they lived why sum chose to go to other contraries and other stead were they were. You may not like what you fine but again you could that's what makes life interesting. I know I am glad I am getting to know about all my ancestors and I am sure you are to. We love them all for them. None of us are perfect we all have our faults, and make mistakes, but if we do our best our Ancestors will be proud of us in the future.

No (1) The Haywood Families Down the Generations

Father Frederick, William, Haywood born June 9, 1836 in Droitwich, England.

Father James, Haywood, Wife Charlotte, Bruton they were married November 12 1835 in Doverdate, Worcester England.

This Family had five children.

1. Frederick William Haywood born 1876 in Doverdate, Worcester, England. Died May 14, 1948 in Toronto Ontario Canada.
2. Louise, Haywood born in Doverdate, Worcester England.
3. James Haywood born Doverdate, Worcester England.
4. Eli Haywood born Doverdate Worcester England.
5. Mill borough Haywood born Doverdate, Worcester England.

We though he was an only child it also open up sum more.

As I went back I come across some more of his family. One of his uncle's, Frederick William Haywood born Birmingham Warwick England. His wife was Eleanor Green born in Birmingham Warwick England. They were married on May 11, 1856.

Number (2) Frederick William Haywood

He originated from Doverdate, Worcester England.

Frederick was born in 1876, to his father James Haywood. Drverdate England. Wife Charlotte, Bruton. Married November 12, 1835 in Doverdate Worcester England. They had 5 children

1. Frederick, William, Haywood, born 1876, in Doverdate, Worcester, England.
2. Louise, Haywood, Doverdate, Worcester, England.
3. James, Haywood, born Doverdate, Worcester, England.
4. Eli, Haywood, born Doverdate Worcester England.
5. Mill, Borough, Haywood born Doverdate, Worcester, England.

We though he was an only child, but it opened up sum more as I went back. then I come across more of his family. One of his uncle's Frederick, William, Haywood, born Birmingham, Warwick, England. Married May 11, 1856. They had 10 children, which we don't know much about.

1. Lucy, Charlotte, Haywood, born April 4, 1858.
2. Marian, Ellen, Haywood, born October 1859.
3. Frederick, William, Haywood, born August 14, 1861.
4. Emest, Haywood, born April 26,1863.
5. James, Haywood, born November 27, 1864.
6. Rose, Haywood, born May 8,1868.
7. Arthur, Emest, Haywood, born May 28,1868.
8. Jessie, Haywood, born May 8, 1870.
9. Frank, Haywood, born September 8, 1872.
10. Charles, Richard, Haywood, born November 9, 1874.

All children were born in Birmingham, Worcester, England.

Later on my grandfather he did join the navy and had a parrot called poly.

He did marry Annie Roberts, and they had three children. They came to Canada with their two children Richard Haywood born 1907, and their daughter Doris Haywood born 1910. Frederick family arrived in Canada in a city called Sorel Quebec on May 8, 1904 on a Vessel Bavarian Port of arrival Montreal Quebec Port of Departure Liverpool England Roll T-82. Their second son was born his name was Frederick William Haywood on December 16, 1907 in Sorel Quebec. Benign in a new country and having a new start they called him after his dad. They lived in Sorel till Frederick was 6 or 7 then moved to Toronto Ontario Canada. They had purchased a three story house on Parliament Street in downtown Toronto Ontario Canada. Each floor was complete for a family to live in. Grampa Haywood found work at Canada Packers, were he work very hard. He was a tall thin man with no hair. He worked their tell retirement came. He was known as a very strict man I guess that come with being in the navy. I remember going to their house and we had to sit very quite on the chesterfield well the news was on. When it came the day for him to retire, he drove into work and dropped off the fellows that drove with him, then went and parked the car. That is when he died November 15, 1969 at the age 89. They said he was worried about retiring. In those days they were not afraid of work, and coming to a new country did what they could to support their families. We love you Grampa and we are glad you are in our family. My you rest in peace.

Memories of Frederick William Haywood
by Evelyn Friend(Haywood) granddaughter.

The Haywood's

Father Frederick, William, Haywood born 1876 died 1948.
Wife Annie Roberts born 1879 died 1968.

(1) Child Richard Haywood born1909 died 2000.
(2) Child Doris Haywood born1910 died 1980.
(3) Child Frederick, William, Haywood born1907 died 1990.

3, The Haywood Family

Father, Frederick, William, Haywood, Born 1876, Birmingham, Warwick, England, Died May 14, 1948 Toronto Ontario Canada,

Wife, Annie, Roberts, Born May 1879 Liverpool, Lancashire England Died November 15, 1968 Toronto Ontario Canada,

Children, Richard, Haywood Born 1909, Liverpool, Lancashire, England, Died 2000 Toronto Ontario Canada,

Doris, Haywood Born 1910, Liverpool Lancashire, England, Died 1980 Toronto Ontario Canada,

Frederick, William, Haywood Born December16, 1907 Sorel, Quebec, Canada, Died October 14, 1990.

This is my grandfather Frederick, William, Haywood and family.

We now go into my grandmother Family.

The Roberts, Generation

Father, John Roberts, age 65 Born in 1881 Liverpool, Lancashire, England, census. Wife, Jane, age 57, Born in 1881 Liverpool Lancashire, England,

Children Edward, Roberts Born in 1846 Liverpool, Lancashire, England,

Thomas Roberts, age 30, Born in 1881 Liverpool, Lancashire, England. Father Edward, Roberts Born December 06, 1846, Liverpool, Lancashire, England. England.

Wife, Alice, Hayes, Born 1812 Liverpool, Lancashire, England, Died 1880 England,

Children Alice, Roberts, age 06 Liverpool, Lancashire, England, Annie, Roberts Born May 1879, Liverpool, Lancashire, England, Died November 15,1968 Toronto, Ontario, Canada,

David, Roberts age 02 Liverpool, Lancashire, England,

Evan Roberts, age 08 Liverpool, Lancashire, England.

Brother and Sister to Edward Roberts, John Roberts, age 65 Liverpool, Lancashire, England. Jane, Roberts age 57 Liverpool, Lancashire, England.

This is all the Roberts family.

4, Annie Roberts and her Family.

Annie Roberts was born in 1879 in Liverpool Lancashire England. In the 1891 England Census I found her family.

Her father was Edward Roberts born 6th of December 1846, he was 43 years old. Mother was Alice Roberts born 1812 she was 39 died 1880. She had a sister Alice Roberts age 6 in 1891, brother David Roberts age 2 in1891, Evan Roberts age 8 in1891, four children in all. Marie L Clarke lived with them to but I don't think she was related. I wish I knew more. There is a lot of Roberts but it's just finding the connection. I did get to know my gamma Annie Roberts; she was a kind gentle lady, who loved children. Annie worked very hard keeping their three story house clean as well raising their three children. I remember it well. As you entered in the front door and on the right was the parlor with a piano it had a roller on top. We use to love to play the songs. On the main floor was the bed room and living room where they watched TV and we had a visit. Then the big kitchens were Polly the parrot sat in his cage. Polly could talk and would say, come on Doris hurry up and do the dishes. We would get a real laugh from him. They had a small back yard with a garage. She always had a small bowl with candy in it for the children. I remember taken my children there and she would give them sum candy from the bowl. She would tell us lots of stories Of the Plains of Abraham which was in Montreal Quebec. She never talked about her family in England. Before Christmas she would gather all of the girl's favored doll and have the lady that lived upstairs on the third floor who worked for Eaton's Canada on making out fits for dolls. After grandpa Haywood died grandma would have me Evelyn and her cousin Barbra who lived upstairs, have a sleep over. We would sleep in grandpa's bed. Before we would go to sleep grandma would read us sum stories from the Bible following the stories we would have a kneeing prayer.

Those were very special times for us. Annie was a small lady with a big hart. She always made you feel welcome. I will never forget her we love you grandma and are so glad you are in our family, may you rest in peace.

Memory's of Annie Roberts.
By Evelyn Friend (Haywood)

No 5, Fred & Mary's Farm.

Frederick, William, Haywood and Mary, Minnie, Gurney. In their years.(1907-1990) (1908-1991) Frederick met Mary two years after she came to Canada. He was working at Canada Packers in Toronto. And she was working for a family named Wile's. A little story about Mary, Minnie, Gurney. She came from Londonderry, North Ireland by boat the Duchess of Bedford at the age of 21. Mary grow up in a family of seven children and a mother Sarah Wallace and father William Gurney. Her mother worked in a factory and her dad was a baker, so Mary had to help out with things at home. She said many a night she did the dishes and other things with her books up in front of her. As she got older she thought that if she would marry and have children she would like more for them. So she heard about people going abroad and decided to come to Canada. Her family was very upset for young ladies didn't do things like that. She was sponsored by a family called Wiles, she work for them for five years to pay off her passage. She met Fred around that time she was sending money back home to help pay the bills. Fred wanted to marry her. But she said not till I pay off my mother's bills. He said I will help you. But she said know it's my responsibly. They did get married five years from then. September 22,1934 and they had a good life together. It was 65 years. They worked side by side on everything to make a good life for them and their children. Evelyn Haywood, Frederick, William, Haywood JR. And Robert, James, Haywood. They had a three bedroom home which they bout off his mom and dad for $3000 dollars. They worked together and fixed it up and built a barn at the end the bottom of the yard. We had a cow named Daisy and she had a cafe named snow ball. We also had five goats, turkeys, chickens, and three horses, rabbets Plus a dog and cat. We found a baby skunk once and tried to give it a bottle, but it died. Mom would put the chick up stairs in brooders to keep them warm so they would grow in the winter, dad would hitch up the red slay we had with a horse and take kids for a ride. Dad just loved all the kids he was in his glory when the kids were around. He would play with them and try to get them to speak French. He also had a small bowl of candy, for the children like his mother. Fred also love music he used to play the banjo he had two of them one had gold around if he would play for mom we used to kid him about it. He was a happy guy. I think he was like his mother; she was the same easy going. But If you were in trouble with him he would talk with you but that was the end he never brought it up again. Fred and Mary were like book ends they know each very well but, she was the boss ask anyone. Under it all she had a soft hart she would make up a bed for the dog or cat or when she would save sum food for them. Our Rose-Anna is like her one day I said to her guess what I know she said I am turning into gamma. David is so like his grandfather. So is my brother Jim Dad will never die with them around. All our children enjoyed their times with them. We use to go down to the farm every summer. Sum times the older boys would be there with their grandparents for the summer. Ron, Dave, and Mike were there when my mother Mary took a stroke, down her left side. She was standing in the kitchen peeling potatoes when it happened, Fred had his back to her watching T.V. Ron came down from up stairs and said are you ok gamma she could not answer him. He knew something was wrong, he was 12 at the time, he called to grampa and he came, took one look and past out. David the second son came down and saw his gamma and past out. Mike the third son came down and looked and Ron give a kick and said don't you dare pass out. Well Mike stead with Mary Ron phone 911 to get help. Mary told everyone that Ron saved her life. She was so glad they were there. The boys had many good times with their grandparents and Fred & Mary with them. Later on Mary went in hospital, and Fred would go to visit every day. One day the nurse phone me in Toronto, and said Evelyn your dad hasn't been in for three days, did he go away sum were. I said no he would not lever my mother. She told me that they had phone the police and they had the dogs out looking. The front door to the house was locked and the car was in the garage. I phoned my brothers Fred & Jim Haywood, we all went down there, as Rose-Anna my daughter and I drove down the road to the farm we saw them coming out of the bush with the dogs. They said they found him. It looked like he had gone down to the back of the farm to look for the cows, and had a cigarette, then took off his cap put it under his head and fell asleep on a log. The hard thing was to tell Mary, Fred, Jim, and Evelyn went to the hospital, as she saw us coming down the hall she new, and said he died, we said yes mom. It was a very sad time for everyone. At his funeral there was so many people it was packed inside and out. We knew he had a lot of people he know. Even Canada packers. He died October 14, 1990. A year later Mary died in Toronto Grace Hospital. She always said don't be sad when I die for I will be with your dad. Rose-Anna and I was at moms (Mary) bedside when it happened. She look down at the end of the bed and said O, there you are Fred I was wounding when you would come for me. I know they are together, and that makes me happy. We Love you. A little story about Mary Minnie Gurney, and Frederick Haywood. She came from Londonderry North Ireland by boat the Duchess of Bedford at the age of 21. Mary grow up in a family of seven children and mother Sarah Wallace and dad William Gurney. Her mother worked in a factory and her dad was a baker, so Mary had to help out with things at home. She said many a night she did the dishes and other things, with her books up in front of her. As she got older she thought that if she was to marry and have children, she would like more for them. So she heard about people going abroad and decide to come to Canada, her family was very upset, for young ladies didn't do things like that. She was sponsored by a family called Wiles, she had to work for them for five years to pay off her passage. She meets Fred, around that time she was sending money back home to help pay the bills. Fred wanted to marry her but she said not till I pay off my mother's bills. He said I will help you. But she said know it's my responsibly. They did get married five years from then. In September 22, 1934 and had a good life together. They worked side by side on everything to make a good life for them self's and their children. Dad always worked hard at Canada Packers and around the house. They had a 3 bedroom house which they bought from his father and mother for $3000 dollars. They had worked together and fixed it up and built a barn at the bottom of the yard. They had three children Evelyn Haywood, Frederick, William, Haywood, Robert, James, Haywood. We had a cow named daisy, and she had a cafe name snow ball. We also had five goats, Turkeys, chickens and three horses, also a big garden. Mom would put the chick up stairs in brooders to keep them warm so they could grow. In the winter dad would hick up the red slay we had with a horse and take kids for a ride. Dad just loved all the kids. He was in his glory when the kids were around he would play with them and try to get them to count and speak in French. He also had a bowl of candy for the children. Fred also loved music he uses to play the banjo, he had two of them one had gold around it he would play for mom, and we use to kid him about it. He was a happy guy I think he took after his mother she was the same, easy going, but if you were in trouble with him he would tell you but that was the end of it, it was never broth up again. Fred and Mary were like book ends they knew each other very well but she was the boss ask anyone. Under it all she had a soft hart, she would make a bed for the dog or cat, or when she would cook save sum for them. She would say don't worry I haven't forgot you. Our Rose-Anna is like her, one day I said guess what, I know she said I am turning into gamma. David our son is so like his granddad Fred Haywood. All of our children enjoyed their time with them, I am so glad they had the opportunity to do so. We all love you both and miss you. My you rest in peace. Memories of Frederick & Mary Haywood by Evelyn Friend (Haywood) Daughter.

No 6, Richard and Margery Haywood and Family.

Richard Haywood was born in 1907 in England to Frederick William Haywood and Annie Roberts. He came to Canada as a little boy. When he grows up he had his own business. He did marry Margery we always called her aunt Margery never knew her last name. They had two daughters Carol and Marin both had red hair. They both married Carol married Jack Watt's and they had a boy and girl, they did divorce. Marin did marry Jim and had two girls. Don't know his last name. He did die. She remarried again don't know who. When Richard their father retired he took up growing flowers, he had a place in a green house where he grows Okras and other flowers. He looked so much like his dad you would think it was. The same built to the balled head. He died in 2000 age 89 in Toronto Ontario Canada.

Both he and Margery are resting in peace. We love you both may you rest in peace.

By Evelyn Haywood (Friend)

No 7, Doris Haywood and Murray Johnson and family.

Doris Haywood was born in England in 1910 to Frederick William Haywood and Annie Roberts. When she grow up she married Murray Johnson. They had one little girl called Barbra Johnson. They lived upstairs at the grandparents house. Barbra did marriage to Billy Guarder and had three boys and one girl.

They live in Ajax Ontario Canada. When Billy was young he had a job at washing windows in high places, and fell to the grown and broke all his bones. Till Billy got better Barbra went to work in real-estate and did very well. Their children are grown and married. Her mother died I am not sure when but it was in Toronto Canada and her dad two. May they both rest in peace.

Memories By Evelyn Haywood (Friend)

No 8, Frederick, William, Haywood Jr.

Fred was Born February 13, 1938, in Toronto Ontario Canada.

He was Fred and Mary's second child, Fred as he likes to be called was a kind of wild child, he was always in trouble. He didn't like school; he would get the teacher upset so she would put him in the hall, till his mother got wind of it. Mother went to the school and said, I didn't send my child to school to sit in the hall. Even If I have to sit behind him he will learn. And that she did, Fred was a care free person all his life but would come up smelling like a rose. He had a charm for the ladies all his life. Fred did have a business he had 3 trucks he sold hot dog, humbuggers, and other things for many years and did good at it. Fred had a stroke on his right side but he was doing well. Life did ketch up with Fred he died on July 9[Th] 2012

He meet Lila Jean Snelling born February 27, 1937, in Toronto Canada. He had gotten her with child, and it was not good around home. They were married for they were so sure that was what they wanted. They were 16 at the time, and both parents had to sine. Then Frederick William was born, January 03, 1957 in Toronto Ontario Canada. Later on they had a girl Julie, born 1960, who has grown up and has a family, plus is running a business of her own. They had another child called Gaven, he had grown up and had a family, and he died of cancer. Fred also has sum grand children, families is, father Edward Allen born 1948 wife Julie Haywood born 1960. Children Bobie-Jo Turkey born 1978. Chantelle, Elizabrth, Turkey born 1989. Melvin, Steve, Kevin, Turkey born 1990. Father Christopher, George, Gross born 1976. Wife Bobbie-Jo Turkey born 1978. Children Irelynn, Patrica, Chantelle, Grossnborn 2002. Jullia, Isabella, Renne, Gross born 2004. Father George Peters. Wife Stacey, Lyn, Haywood born 1990, cildrenAlison, Lila, Rose, Peters born 2011. Austin, Max, Garvin, Peters born 2012. Father George, Garvin, Haywood born 1987. child Mackenzie, Elizabeth, Irene, Haywood born 2012. Fred son Garvin born1961 and died 1998 wife Irene Garnett married 1984 children George, Garvin, Haywood born 1987. Stacey, Lyn, Haywood born 1990. I hope I got them all. Fred and Lila did divorced. Fred meet Audrey Lorraine Willer born April 10, 1945 in Newfoundland Canada. She died of Cancer, October 12, 2007 in Whibty Ontario Canada. They had a son called Shawn born July 03, 1984. Shawn did very well he went to school and become a computer exert, and a computer company, called I B M. ask him if he would work for them. They played his school and his room and food. He has to work for them for five years. Sum Company does that if they see a student who is good at what they do. We wish you luck Shawn. And we are glad you are all in our family.

Memories of Fred Haywood & family
By Evelyn Friend (Haywood) Sister.

No 9, Robert James Haywood and Lynda Jane Darraugh and Family.

Robert James Haywood was born December 26 1942 to Frederick William Haywood and Mary Gurney. Jim as he was called was a quite boy, who did very well for himself. After high school he got a job with a company. But after a while it had to down size so he took another one. He also worked for Ward's funeral home. He meets Lynda Jane Darraugh born September 27 1943, they went together for a well then Jim ask her to marry him. Jim went to his Mother and Dad to let them know they were getting married, and mom said to him you know Jim there are two kinds of woman, one is a career and the other is a home maker. And Lynda is a career woman. He said that's ok. They did marry October 22 1965. And they had a little girl her name is Lorie Ann, Haywood born July 18 1976. She is the apple of their eye. Jim was very close to her and help teach her a lot of life skills. Lorrie writes children books. And got married to, Ted Hutchison born December 16. They had two children Cooper, James, Hutchson born August 22, 2008 and Molly Elizabeth, born October 4 2012.

Jim and Lynda are retied now in Collingwood and enjoy their grand children. We love you all and are glad you are in our family.

By Evelyn Haywood (Friend) sister.

Evelyn Haywood Friend (2001)

Evelyn Haywood born July 18, 1936, in Toronto, Ontario, Canada to Frederick William Haywood & Mary Minnie Gurney.

Evelyn was born with a cleft pellet and a hair lip, it was a bad one, when mom first saw me she said my poor baby, first she thought it was her fault, but it wasn't. They didn't have much money but when she found out that I could have sum operations to fix my lip and other parts, she went up to ask if she could borrow the money, she then begged them and said I promos I will pay back sum every week if you would lend it to me. They didn't have OHIP, It wasn't ease growing up in the 50's people worked hard for their families. Everyone had a garden and we had sum chickens and other things to keep us going. I liked our neighbourhood, people were ones to look out for each other, no one every locked their door. It was like one big family. If someone was sick everyone would help out. That was when the bread was deliver, I remember when we had a pony called poly, she was old, mom use to put my brother Jim on her back and poly would take him all over the naberhood every morning and bring him home. One day when poly was out by herself she walked into a friends front porch and ate the loaf of bread that the bread man left. We all had a good laugh. People didn't get upset back then the same. I had a good child hood. And to good and loving parents; I was the apple of my dad's eye. I did the boy thing dating, we would go in groups most times Later on I did get married on May 18,1945, we were married in the ST John's church in the town of Weston were I grow up in. It was 100 years old the week before we got married. My husband was Ronald peter Simpson born August 04, 1935 in Montreal Quebec Canada. His mother was a sweet lady. His dad had died. We had 09 children. I am sorry to say we did get a divorce. I was happily married to William John Friend, who died June 20, 2012. And between us we have 10 children & 16 grand children, and 6 grates grand children, Bill had one and I had 09. We love and enjoy them all; it's lots of fun when they come to visit. We are so blessed having the family we have, we love you all, Bill passed away on June 20 2012 he was a great husband and friend, Evelyn, Haywood, Friend.

By Evelyn Friend (Haywood)

No 11, Ronald, Peter, Simpson Jr.

Ronald, Peter, Simpson was born August 05, 1958 in London Ontario Canada. His mother is Evelyn Haywood and his father is Ronald, Peter, Simpson. Ron was a good baby, he was very smart to, and Ron walked at 10 months old. He was a quite child and a loner. He did well in school, in high school he liked to take pictures and was very good at it. He took a picture of our family; he set it up then got in it to. Ron did marry Micheal but it didn't work out. He lives in Calgary Alberta Canada and loves it there. Ron has done well for himself, he did have his own business with a friend but his friend died. So he is working in an office now, it's for a plumbing business called Joes Plumbing. We love and miss him, but one has to go were the work is.

We love you Ron and we are glad you are in our family.

Memories of RON Simpson
By Evelyn Friend (Haywood) Mom.

No 12, David and Heidi Simpson and Family.

James David is the second child of Ronald, Peter Simpson and Evelyn Haywood. David was born December 14, 1959 in Quebec City Canada. He was 4lbs 9oz, and he Nelly died three times on us. Dave was a strong baby, in his younger years; he participated on different sports team like football, basketball, baseball, and hockey. His first love in sports is hockey and favourite team is the Montreal Canadians.

He was always close with his family. Sports and growing up in a large family helped develop a great work ethic, which has continued throughout Dave's life today. Education has been an ongoing process to Dave works for B.Y.U. in the printing area as well as a Photographer and graphic designer on the side. He just got a gold award for a book he did called Finding a Safe Harbor. Once he come in first with doing a slogan for a company. Enjoys the outdoors work, puttering and hanging out with the family. He has done very well for himself and his family. The love of his life is Heidi. I believe this saying "behind every good man is a great women" Dave did marry on August 23, 1986 in Manti, Sanpete Utah Temple, U.S.A. We love you and are glad you are in our family.

Heidi Anderson was born March 21 1961 in Nephi Juab Utah, U.S.A. With her mother Linda Peel and Earl Dean Anderson, who taught the value of honesty and hard work. She also had two sister and two brothers. They all lived by the quote "if it's worth doing it's doing it right." Heidi dad said "I may not be rich but my wealth is in my kids. Heidi is trying to pass these grate traits on to her daughters Lindsey and Rylli. Heidi works for Utah Valley Community credit union as a Mortgage underwriter. She has a passion for running and trying to stay in shape. Enjoys working in the yard and making quilts. The time she spends with the girls Lindsey and Rylli is considered a great treasure. Heidi is also a great wife to my son Dave, and a great daughter in law. She shows a great example to everyone. We love you Heidi and we are so glad you are in our family.

Lindsey, Nicole, Simpson was born December 29 1988, in Greenville, South Carolina, U.S.A. Lindsey is a quite young lady. When she was in her last year of high school, she took a cores to be a pharmacy helper and did very well. She also work at a drug store. Linz as we call her has a zest for life and always is working on something new. Her Interests include playing the piano, she also tot it, running and playing tennis. Lindsey has recognized the value of having great friends, she has been strengthen by good examples. Education has been important to Lindsey as well. She has her Masters now, and is going for another Master one in a difference part of her field She has learned her lessons, "line precept upon precept." Her relationship with Rylli is close. They help push each other to do better. We love you Lindsey, Keep up the good work. Lindsey is engaged to be married on August 27 2013, to Ryan Nielsen. We all wish you both lose of happiness. And we are so glad you are in our family.

Rylli Mckell Simpson born December 18 1996 in Murray Salt Lake Utah U.S.A. Rylli is a very outgoing young girl. Just full of life. She has found following in an older sister footsteps is sometimes difficult. She is gaining her own identity. Rylli was in junior high but now is in high school. She enjoys playing the piano and singing. She also teach piano. Rylli Sang in the Mormon, Tabernacle Quire with other young people in salt Lake City. Sum times she helps her dad in his shop. And she also baby sits. We wish we had her energy. Rylli has high expectations and holes to her conviction. She did summer school to help her grades for high school. Rylli also loves doing hair styles and cosmetics things. She would like to do arrangements for Weddings, and things It is called a even planer. She is doing her sister Lindsey wedding. Rylli will be taken schooling to do all that is involved in that line. We love you Rylli and keep up the good work, as she is always on the go. We are so glad you are in our family.

By Evelyn Haywood (Friend) Gramma.

No 13, Micheal Bradly Simpson and Family.

Micheal Bradly Simpson was born February 18 1961 in Loretteville Quebec Canada. Mike as he likes to be called was a good boy. But did like to get into things. One day he pushed a chair to the kitchen counter and climbed up on it then onto the fridge he wasn't even walking, another time I put a pail on the table to call out the window to the other two boys to get back here and I hadn't even got my head back in and he claimed up on the table and drank the water with soap and jovial. My friend and I phone the base ambulance write away. They said he has to drink milk and he won't, I said give it to me and pored it down him he was ok, he was always doing things like that. When we lived in Webbwood Michael help along with his brothers Dave and Ron help to build the house. He also chop wood for the fire in the winter. Mike built a nice coffee table for the living room in shop at school. When he left home he went to Mississauga for work. He got a job at K mark he had a few jobs. He now works for Home Hardware in Oshawa on where he works. He did marry Joy Maria Campbell in Toronto.

They had two lovely boys Mark Daniela Simpson and Nicholas Brady Simpson. Mike and Joy did divorce and Mike got coasty for both boys. It took a well he had to go down to Quebec every other week end for he was working. He had to spend time so the children aid could how thing were going. It wasn't easy. But he did a great job raising the two boys. They have turn out to be two fine boys and we are grateful for that. Mike is on his own now and has a cat. We love you Mike and are glad you are in our family.

Mark Daniel Simpson born November 14, 1983 in Oakville On Canada. Mark has a little girl Danni Laura Simpson, born September 16, 2010 in Brampton On. Canada. Her mother is Amanda, Gibb who was born August 22,1984 in Whibty Ontario Canada. They didn't marry but both are raising their little girl.

Which is 3 in September.

Nicholas Bradley Simpson born September 2, 1985 in Oakville Ontario Canada. Nick as he likes to be called was a sweet loving baby, who grew to be a loveable well manned young man. He loves people and gets along with everyone. He is working in a cambial plant. He went on a safety core for his work. It can be very dangers if one is not carful. He hops to go back in the further. We hope that happens. He bought a new car and is doing well. He also has been going with a girl named Jesus. And they are engaged to marry. Nick went to her dad and said I would like to marry your daughter and I would like to have your blessing. He said you can marry my daughter and have our blessing. He then told her they were going out to dinner. She was getting her jewelry on and that is when he asks her to marry him. She was so surprised and said what you really are asking, she said Yes. Jesus is a lovely girl. We wish you both all the happiness and best in the world. And we love you both.

By Evelyn Haywood (Friend) Gramma.

No 14. Brenda-Lyn Simpson, David White & Family

Brenda-Lynn Tina-Louse Simpson Born March 30,1965, in Toronto Ontario Canada. Brenda was a small baby she was 3lbs 12ozs, she was an 8 mouth baby. They had her on enfarlack milk with iron. She did not like it, she would push it out with her tongue. I told them to change the milk, they wouldn't, she had to have the iron. You couldn't tell them. One night we were looking at the baby's, and a man went in to fix the incubator with greasy over all, s, I said that is it I am taken my baby home. They tried to stop me and said she would die. I said I just have to try. I tried her on the milk and she wouldn't take it. Then I give her water she almost ate the bottle. So I got her farmer wife number 2, and as soon as she knew it wasn't the same, she was fine.

I rented scales to keep an eye on her wait. The doctor's office had phoned ask how the baby was doing. I said she is up to 10 lbs. She was in shock. Brenda has turned out to be a lovely lady. I had waited for a girl and after 3 boys I wasn't going to lose her if it was possible. She was always a happy girl, and very parlour with the boys. Brenda took Ballet lessons, she was in a concord and it was named The Birds. They looked so cute in their costumes and dancing around. She was a thoughtful girl and was close with her family. She tries to keep in touch with each one. But been a gamma now it keeps her busy, with answering there questions and doing things with them and visits. Brenda you are a good parson and good mother, you are very thoughtful and we love you for it. She did marry, David John White Born February, 15, 1963 in Sudbury Ontario Canada. They have two lovely girls, Natalie-Ann Patrice-Lynn Born March 02, 1983, Sudbury Ontario Canada. She is working with women and helps them get their lives in order and loves it. She has a boy friend Chris Brassard, she has been going with him for a long time. They have a baby girl she was born May 30, 2013 weight 7lbs 14oz. Her name will be Lily Brassard and we wish them good luck. They will have lots of stories to tell us in the further.

Natalie put herself through school; she always had good marks and got a scholar ship to 5 universities. She is doing great; Natalie was always a go getter. She always had two jobs. And has decided to go back to school She has really done very well for herself. Keep up the good work Nat, and we love you. And we are so glad you are in our family.

Christine White was born December 14, 1984, Christine went back to school and took a Corse in charted accounting. She now manages a Subway Restraint and does the books. Christine you are doing well with all you have on your plate, keep up the good work. Christine is a single mother to Seth David Alexsander White, who was born December

06,2004, Seth will be attending grade 3. He is in French aversion, and is doing well he loves music, I sent him a player and soon children songs, and he would say to anyone come and listen to my music, he likes to watcher's Spiderman. Seth Father is Mark, Emile, Berthraume, Born November 01,1984. Sactera, Brenda, Alexandra, White. Born August 06, 2007, Sactera attending grade 1 and likes to watch Dora, and sing songs. Her Father is Shannon Bourque. Born October27, 1989. We love you Christine, Seth and Sactera and we are so glad you are in our family.

Memories of Brenda, Natalie, Christine
By Evelyn Friend (Haywood)

No 15, Thomas, Jeffrey, Steven, Simpson

Thomas Jeffrey Steven Simpson Born March 20, 1967 Midland Ontario Canada. Tom was a good baby he was born on a Thanks given week-end, I was just going to have my dinner and it happened, he was the biggest baby I had almost 7 lbs. He was very good with making bikes, He had a paper route once. Tom was into running he got so many trophies and meddles, One year he got student of the year and all round sports. He got cross country. People used to say he runs like a deer. He gives me sum and I got them framed. We love you Tom, and wish the best for you. And are glad you are in our family.

Memories of Tom Simpson
By Evelyn Friend (Haywood) Mom.

No 16. Melvina-May Bonnie-Lynn Simpson

Born May 31,1969, Born Kona Ontario Canada. Melvine was adopted at the age of eight she had three brothers from her other family. When she came to us she didn't know how to do anything, it was hard adjusting to a new family. The other children were very good in accepting her as one of the family. Melvina did get married to Author Collette, and has two children Candace Collette and Kayla Collette They living up in Sudbury sad to say we don't keep in touch. We hope you are doing fine. And are glad you are in our family.

Memories of Melvina & Arthur Collette & family.
By Evelyn Friend (Haywood)

No 17. Jonathan, Dean, Andrew, Simpson.

Jonathan, Dean, Andrew, Simpson was Born
January29, 1973, in Sudbury Ontario Canada.
Died January 31, 1973, Sudbury Ontario Canada.

Jonathan was a Lovely, happy baby, when he was in the incubator he would hit the breathing cup up high and smile. It was if he was telling us he was happy. But when I got back to my room they said he has died. It was a real shock. Jonathan came to this earth for a name and a blessing, which he got.

We Love you Jonathan and we are so glad you are in our family.

May you rest in peace?

Memories of Jonathan Simpson
By Evelyn Friend (Haywood)Simpson) Mother.

Daniel Geary Joseph Simpson

Born Feb 15, 1972, Sudbury Ontario, Canada. Dan is thoughtful, he never for gets a birthday. Dan went to school to become a big wheel trucker, he past and is driving for snider. He loves driving so he might as well get paid for it. Dan had a lot of things he was alertest to when he was growing up. It was 24 mostly food. He had to have a different meal from everyone else. He has out grown them now. Dan has two children now, and is very lucky. One 17 years and will be 18 on July 14th.

Her name is Mariah Daniella Simpson Born July 14, 1993, Toronto Ontario Canada. She was born in Toronto, but her mother Val wanted to go back home and take her with her. Mariah lives in Saskatchewan Alberta with her mom.

She has been looking for her dad for 10 years and others in her family. Rose-Anna found her on face book. She said she was so happy she found us that she cried, she said you have no idea how It feel. I had a not in my stomach. She is 5'4, and has natural auburn hair and baby blue eyes, she is taken cosmetology, and some business classes, She is in grade 12 this year, and will be graduating and going to Medicine Hat in Alberta. Mariah wrote I know all of you have missed part of my life, but I still have lots of years to share with you all. I would very much like to meet all of you one day. You will always be a part of my life from now on. She did come and meet everyone I ask her would you like to be in my book. She said I would love to be in it. I always thought of her over the years and Id wonder how she was doing. She said Thank-you for keeping me in your heart. Well Mariah you have a family that dose love you, and we hope you, will always know that. And now we have meet you thanks' to Rose-Anna and face book. We are so glad you are in our family, love gamma.

Dan did marry Maria Carmela Sulmona Born May 9, 1972, Toronto Ontario Canada. They married on May 19.1996,

And had Austin Born June 19,1998, In 2004 Austin was 6 years old and his first sport was soccer, he played for the town of Noble ton /Kleinberg. His team (Municipal Maintenance) they won the championship, in September 2009-April at the age of 11 he joined his first house league hockey team (Maple view) they also won the championship cup. Only at the age of 12 Austin has a most memorable moment which happened on Friday July 9, 2010. He had the opportunity to touch the Stanley cup and personal meet Nicholas Boynton one of the Pittsburgh Penguins player who was raised in Noble ton Ontario Austin just loves all sports. He is doing well in school. He said he wants to be a police man when he grows up. Austin is a delightful boy and is welled mannered. We love you Austin keep up the good work. We love you and are so glad you are part of our family.

Maria (Sulmona) Simpson was born on May 9, 1972. It wasn't till the age of 18 month when her parents were told she had a condition/ disability know as Cerebral Palsy which had occurred at birth. This did not stop her from living a normal life. At the age of 9 she started riding horses once a week as a form of physical therapy. As she got to the age of 18 she was approached by the sports for Disabled committee to ride for the Canadian Dressage Team.1991 she represented Canada in Denmark winning 2 Bronze medals,1994 she represented Canada in England winning a Silver medal,1994 she was part of the Retirement Show at the Royal Winter Fair for Big Ben the horse of Ian Millar the Famous Canadian Jumping Team's Gold medallist,1996 she represented Canada in the first Para-Olympics held in Atlanta placed 6th out of 15. In 1998 she had Austin and took a couple of years off riding.2001 she rode out west in Langley, British Columbia for the national Pacific Rim and came home overall highest score of the entire event and National champion. This event was one that she would never forget. The day she was suppose to come back home was September 11,2001, and due to crisis that occurred that day she was stranded for another 7 days before she could get a flight home back to Woodbridge to see Austin who was 3 years of age and hadn't seen his mother in over 3 weeks. Since that event she decided to take another bred k and is now in the process of trying to get on the Canadian Team. It is not as easy as it use to be to qualify but she actively riding and competition individual. We love you Maria and Dan and Austin and Mariah for your enforces. And are glad you are in our family.

Memories of Dan & Maria& Family
By Evelyn Friend (Haywood)

No 19. Rose-Anna Cindy-Lynn Simpson

Born June 15, 1976 in Sudbury Ontario Canada

Rose-Anna was the cutes baby, and gives me no trouble. She has been a very thoughtful girl all her life. I remember when her brother Dan and sister Melvina decided to sell flowers to people, so they put them in little bounces and tried them up with ribbon, they had Rose-Anna go to the doors and ask if they would like sum flowers, of cores she was dressed in a dress and was so cute that no one could refuses her. When they got back home they didn't want to share with her. Mother said everyone gets the same amount in the money for you all did work for it. They all learned a good lesson that day you have to be fair with each other. She was working for a lawyer and she looked after their little boy Jared and would take a large sum of money to the bank on Fridays also do filling for him. When she was planning to go back to school he asks her to sit in on the interties. She brought her first pay check home and said her mom, I said that is yours. She said you need it more than me. Another time I came home from work and on my bed was a top and skirt for me. She was always thinking of others. She knew she had to be home by 6pm for supper, and would get there just on time. I said to her one day, you always get here just on time and you don't have a watch, how do you do it, she said I ask my friend for I don't want to be late. She had to do the dishes after supper. And her little boy friend said hurry up so we can play. And she said to him if you help me then I will be done faster. When Rose-Anna was little she loved to ride the sled with the dog pulling her in the winter. She also liked to ski and she took finger skating for a few years, and love it. She always had odd jobs. Rose-Anna did married December 07, 1996, and has 4 grate children. Rose-Anna has turned out to be a great wife and supper mom. She also works at a day care, 5 days a week. In September 2013 she will be retuning back to s Collage to be a Developmental Services and Communicative Disorders Assistant. Keep up the good work. Rose-Anna.

Edward George Scea

Born March 14, 1974 in Toronto Ontario Canada

We didn't know Edward when he was grown up, but he came from a family of six children and a mother and dad. We have gotten to know him better now. When he ask Rose-Anna for her hand in mirage, she said to him before that happens you have to go and take with my mother, for that is the way we do things in our house, he said ok. Edward came to me and said I believe you have to take to me if I want to marry Rosa-Anna We did have a take and he asks me what I expected of him. I said I expected you to finish, your schooling and if Rosa-Anna wants to do the same to support her, plus work to prove a roof for you to. And never lay a finger on her every, He said yes her brothers will fix me. No I said I will be the one. To always love her. I can say Edward has lived up to all his prompts. He is a good husband and father. Edward went to Toronto University, U.F.T. and graduated with a Bachelor of Science with a Specialist in Psychology. He works at The Meta Centre as a supportive Independent living councillor. He helps individuals with Developmental disabilities, live in the community he assists them with all aspects of their lives that need help with. Keep up the good work, Edward.

Hannah Kennedy Scea

Born September 06, 1997 Blessing Oct. 12, 1997 Baptism September 18, 2005. Hannah was the first child of Rosa-Anna & Edward Scea. From the day she was born we fell in love with her. Hannah has gone through a lot in her years of life, with all her operations, and speech, she was born with a clef. And she has had to overcome a lot. She dose try, but its hard sum times. When gamma was out there for a week once, I saw her bike in the garage, and said Hannah it's time you learned to ride your bike, she said but I can't gamma. I said you can I will help you. She said ok. But first we have to say a prayer, so heavenly Father will help you. So we did, we tried first time It didn't work. But the next time she was off like she had been always riding it for a long time, to her surprise. She said look gamma. I can do it. When her mom and dad come home they saw her go by them on her bike. And were so happy she could ride it. She can play a song on the piano. And volunteer's at her school with the little ones outside when they are out play en, and other things and loves it. Hannah's teacher though she deserves something, so she wrote to the government and they sent her a medal it is citizen ship medal. This medal is not given out very often. At graduation it's a big deal the girls have a nice dress on and have their hair done to go up on the stage to revive their diploma. She loves to be with her friends. She dose jobs around the house. Also dose volunteer at the pet store. And is enjoying high school, after high school she will be in collage. Hannah is a very good at drawing free hand, and crafts. She looks forward to going to the EX it's a big fair that is in Toronto every August to September. She loves to go with gamma. It's a day to spend to gather haven fun. Keep up the good work Hannah.

Joel Edward Seth William Scea

Joel was born Oct. 18, 2003, at St Michael hospital, in Toronto Ontario.

He is a very good at learning things. He has a saying if you ask him can I help you Joel, he said no Joel will do it. He is very independent. And while mannered, I was at his church one Sunday, and everyone was chatting, and all of a sudden this little voice said everyone this is my grammar. We were surprised; I said thank-you Joel for interdosing me. I had them out one day to Mc Donald's for lunch, and there was some men working outside. I said Joel come and eat he said grammar I have to whack them work so I can learn how to do it, so we ended up sitting by the window. When he gets a present from me he said look what my grammar give me isn't it nice. That was the year he started school I give him pencils' and a sharpener and a few other things, I though he wouldn't like it. For his eight birthdays he got some real tools, and when he opened it he was so excited he grab my legs and said thank you grammar& papa He tells everyone I got real tools. No matter what he gets he is happy. When Joel and grammar go to the EX, the Toronto fair he likes to go and visit the arm force. They have tanks, plains, and he likes to do the sit ups and the over and under and the mass, and the bars, one hand then the other, the man said to him when he got to the bars, do you need help he said no I will do it. They time them when they go through the excise, and he did it in 3 minutes. Then did it again.

The plains are his favoured he was asking lots of questions. And the air man could see he wanted to learn so he took the time with Joel, which was nice. Joel is in grade three now, and is very much a leader. He likes to be in control. He is in the scouting program, and loves it. He loves camping, and is taking swimming at school Also he is in brake dancing him and Mary have a recital soon. His mom Rose-Anna Scea says he is my fixes man. Keep up the good work Joel.

Hunter, David, Adam, Scea,

Born Februarys 10,2006 at St Michael Hospital in Toronto Ontario Canada. Hunter is a lovely little boy, with the biggest smile. When he look at you with that smile one could melt. He likes to hide on everyone, and play with you. When he was a little younger his mom put a safety lock on the fridge, to keep him out as she thought. And he would take the lock off and go in the frig and get what he wanted then lock it up again. I was standing there one day when he did it. His mom said I don't know why I bother; he knows how to open it anyway. When Hunter was one and a half we took him berry picking, and the man said not to step on the plants, to go up and down the rolls them across to the next roll, so his mom put him down so she could pick the berries, next thing Hunter took off down the roll to the top and down the next one. At first we thought he was just running away, but he was doing what the man said. Rose-Anna and I said (Grammar) said we don't know what he was doing but he sure does. That's our Hunter; even though he could not take he understood everything. Hunter is in grade one this year, The first day his mom took him in to meet the teacher he took off down the hall and to hide. He has only escaped one more times since. His mom has him in school 3 days a week and the other days in nursery the first year. This year he goes all day every day. She said it's the teacher job now. We were waiting to he gets a litter older before he goes to the EX, and in the year 2012 he got to go. This year Hunter got a wood set so he can build things he loved it. Boy's need to be busy with their hands. He is doing well in school. He too was born with a clef and goes to speech every Friday morning. Keep up the good work Hunter.

Mary, Sarah, Elizabeth, Scea

Mary was born December 19, 2008, at St Micheal Hospital in Toronto Ontario Canada. She had a blessing on January 04 2009. Mary is a bundle of joy; she has pretty curly red hair, and a real going crone. She doesn't miss a thing. And doesn't let her brothers and sister lave her behind. She picks up very fast Mary watches very close to what is done and how it's done. You show her once and she can do it. She is a very clever little girl. One day she was in the kitchen at grammas with the others kids, and I said do you want sum Mary she looked at me and said mm, in other words yes. Mary has a lazy eye and wears glasses to correct it. Her first pare was gold farm and looked so cute. Mary likes to sing and dance and dress up, love to wear everyone's shoes. She is quite the little girl. Mary was in Junior Kindergaden last year for three days a week and every other Friday. She is 04 now but will be 05 on December 19/2013.Starting in September 2012 she will be in school all day every day. She knows her A.B.C. and count numbers and colours very well. She can write her name and also when she sees it she knows it right away. When she is sitting at a desk doing her work she really doesn't let anything or anybody take her away from that. It's not easy being young and having to learn all about how things are done. But Mary is doing so well with everything , she loves her teacher and the other kids, they are all her friends. We don't think she will have any problems. Mary is in Ballard she was on stage with other little girls doing her dance. There were a lot of people which in, the dance but she didn't let that stop her she went ahead and did the hole dance anyway. It was so nice to be there and see her up on stage she is a real trouper. We love you Mary and we are so glad you are in our family.

Memories of Rose-Anna & Edward, Hannah, Joel, &Mary Scea
By Evelyn Haywood Friend Gamma.

William John Friend

Bill Friend

William was born on January 05, 1937 in Toronto Ontario Canada. He was born to Ena and Albert Friend.

He had a brother named John Leggett Friend. William went to a trade school, named Tec. As he grows up he had many different Jobs. His love is for boats. William would fix boats for people and deliver them; he also had his own boat at one time. He had his own business doing all kinds of things like bikes, moderns; if it could be fixed he could do it. It's the same today. He got a job on the Etobicoke Board of education. He went to school, and got his 4th, 3rd, and 2scented papers for a station engineer. He was a smart man and a hard worker. He is now retired and does the fixing around the house and enjoys all the grand children and grates. We love you William and are glad you are in our family.

Jobs. William had his own business at one time, fixing bikes, boats, and many other things. He use to deliver boats as well for people, and had his own boat. After a while he got haired on the Etobicoke Board of Education While there he went to school and got his 4th, 3rd and 2nd, class engineers papers. He loved working in around children, they would ask him from time to time to fix's their bikes; he would help out where he could. Bill is the type if it could be fixed he can do it, he is the same today. Bill is retired now and the only fixing he douses is around the house and a neighbor. He loves all his grand children, and grates, he is a good parson and we love and are glad you are in our family. Bill died on June 20/2012 and is snarly missed.

Memories of William Friend
by Evelyn Friend Wife

No 21, The Hurry Family Robert, Christine, Mattie & Keith & Tana.

Rob is a great guy; he has a good sense of Humour. And loves his Wife Christine, and two children Madison, and Keith, Rob works for a country as a meat inspector, for the government, he goes around to the farmers and checks the live stock to make sure they are healthy for people to eat before slathering. The famers have to meet the codes of the government. He does a good job. We enjoy his company when he comes with his family.

Christine is a busy wife and mother, with two active kids; she is always on the go taking them to school and to their other actives. She enjoys when we all get together, it's a fun time. Tana was her first born She is on her own now is doing well.

Madison is a delightful little girl. She goes to school, and she likes to play with her dolls and the game battle ship, when ever soon one gives her something she is happy with it, and express joy and said thank-you. Love to play with her mates, and doing different actives like ringgit she is very good at that. They have tremens and play agents other teams.

Keith is a delightful little boy, who loves trains. It is one of his passions. Give him a train and you have a happy camper. He also is into hockey he plays gold tender on his team, and looks good in his gear. We love you all and we are glad you are in our family.

Memories of Christine & Rob & Madison & Keith Hurry
By Evelyn Haywood Friend.

No 22. The Gurney's Wallace's and Carr's

James Gurney born 1877 He was William's Gurney father. His wife was Mary born 1845. Their children is Hugh Gurney, James Gurney. Maggie Gurney. Jane Gurney, Mary Gurney, William Gurney, John Gurney. They had seven.

William Wallace born 1856, his wife was Margaret Carr born 1827. They had two daughters Sarah Wallace born 1871 and died 1952. She was our grandmother. Eliza Wallace.

James Carr his wife was Margaret.

Children Michael Carr, James Carr, Mary Carr, Bridget Carr, Margaret Carr, Edmund Carr, there was six in this family.

No 23. The Gurney's

This is our grandparents and their children.

Father William Gurney Born 1872 and Died 1952.

Wife Sarah Wallace Born 1871 Died 1954, Married 1900 in Londonderry Ireland. Children, James Gurney Born 1903, Died 1925.

Mary Minnie Born 1908 Died1991. Margaret Gurney born1905 died1941.

Lewis Gurney Born 1914 Died 1980.

Evelyn Gurney Born 1921 Died 1988.

William Gurney Born 1910 Died1910.

William Gurney Born 1911 Died 1911.

There was seven they were a hardly group.

No 24. William Gurney

William Gurney was born in Londonderry North Ireland, in 1872.

He was a kind, loving, grandfather who loved his family; His father was James, Gurney and mother was Mary. William was a tall big man. When he was young he joined up in the army and went to war. And while he was fighting there was a lot going on around him, and at one point he was buried for three days alive, but he serviced. William liked to play the horses and gramma would get mad at him, but he never worried about that. William was a baker by trade, and a good one. That is why we are good cooks and baker we take after him. William was so happy when he heard that Mary Minnie Gurney his daughter and her daughter Evelyn were coming for a visit, but in the mean while he had a fell down and broke his hip. He was in hospital when we arrived, but he was so happy to see us. He said to me we are going to have a big party for you when I get out. But in those days they didn't know as much as they know today, and infection set in and he died. It was a sad day for all of us. I was looking forward to spending time with him and getting to know him more. In Ireland in those days the casket was in the house, and the men walked and woman rode. Mary his daughter and Evelyn said we would walk to the grave site. They did have a party, but he was there in spirit. He dies in July 16th, 1952. He married in December 25, 1900, to Sarah Wallace. We all love and miss you,

And are so glad you are in our family. May you rest in peace?

Memories of William Gurney.
By Evelyn Friend (Haywood) Granddaughter.

No 25. Sarah Wallace, Gurney

Sarah Wallace was born in North Londonderry Ireland, in May 1871. Her father was William Wallace and mother was Margaret, Carr, they also had a daughter Eliza, Wallace. That is all we could find. Sarah and William had seven children five lived and two died. They lived in a small house in the Lower road, it had an open fire place where our gamma Sarah did all the cooking and backing, she made the best scones. I only wish I got her recipe. She worked in a factory to help out her family. Sarah came to Canada for a visit to her daughter's Mary's place, one night she had gotten up from supper and she said to Mary I am starved, the children said, how could that be she just ate, mom said she means she is cooled. In Canada it means one is Hungary that was our first translated word. Sarah had the longest long gray hair; it went from the top of her head to the floor. She said it's like that because I take a hole egg and eat it hole, I don't know how much of that is true, she did eat the egg hole, but I know she would brush it out and leave it lose, at night, then in the day would twist it up into a bun for the day. It was just like silk even throw it was gray it was beautiful. She had a kind hart, the Allen children used to visit her and she would give them a meal. There is no food like your granny's. They were very close to her. She was a short stocky woman, and we are so glad you are in our family. My you rest in peace.

Memories of Sarah Gurney (Wallace)
By Evelyn Friend (Haywood) granddaughter.

Allen Family That Have Their Own Tree,

1, Father Robert, Allen Born September27,1902, married1933, Died December10,1986 Ireland, Wife Margaret Gurney BornSeptember10,1905, Died December17,1980 Ireland,

Children Bertie, Allen Born1934 Ireland, William, Lewis, Allen Born June21,1935 Ireland, Mary, May, Allen Born February 05,1937 Ireland, Charlie, Winston, Allen BornJuly12,1942 Ireland, James, Allen Born January06,1938, Ireland, Raymond, Allen BornApril11,1944, Died July 03,2003 Ireland, Elizabeth, Lila, Allen Born August 19,1939Ireland.

Father James Allen Born January 06, 1938, married September17,1986 Ireland, Wife Sarah, Teresa, Rabbit Born June 16,1934 Ireland,

Children Christine, Allen BornDecember16,1965 Germany, Jacqueline Born Octber30,1967 Germany.

Father Charlie, Winston, Allen Born July12, 1942, married Octber23,1969 Ireland, Wife Joyce, Barbara, Whitfield Born September18,1942 England,

Children Anninna, Elizabeth, Allen BornSeptember02,1960 England, married John, Reid March 30,1985

children AmIee Born February 28,1983 England, married Rod, Light September 02, children Luke, Light Born November 24 2000 England, Poppy Light Born December 25,2007 England, Haley light Born December28,1985 England,

children Jamie Born May 30,2004 England, Kelsie Born October 27,2010 England, Natlalie Born September 29,1987. Angela Marie, Allen BornJanuarey24,1962, husband Bryan, Ernest, Steele Born June 27,1954 mairredNovember14,1981 England,

child Gemma, Marie, Steele Born September 30,1982 England, husband James, Ashby England,

children Toa, James, Steele, Ashby Born July 28,2009 England, Aria, Mortimer, Ashby Born October 16,2010 England, Anaheria, Marie, Ashby Born October16,2010 England, Ninnas Born September 02,1960 England, Liam, Charles, Whitfield, Allen BornMarch21,1973 England, Wife Helen Wake Born April 19.1972England, child Nischa Eleanor Allen Born March 12,1995 England.(End)

Father Raymond, Allen Born April11,1944, married January 08,1970, Died March07,2003Ireland, WifeAnn, Mcbride Born May 04,1945Ireland,

Children Donna Allen BornOctber23,1971 Ireland, Bernadette Allen BornDecember30,1973 Ireland, Katherine Allen BornNovember23,1974 Ireland.

Father Michael, Harrison Born July17,1937 Scotland married February 23,1957, Died December26,2009 England, Wife Elizabeth, Lila, Allen Born August 19,1939 Ireland,

Children Stephen Harrison BornFebruary21,1960 England, Paul, Harrison BornJune17,1961 England.

Father William, Norris BornMay24,1937, marriedMarch28,1964 Ireland, Wife Mary, May, Allen Born February 05,1937 Ireland,

Children Robert, James Norris Born September 21,1965 married July 06,1996 Ireland, Wife Caroline, Bennett Born June24,1962 Ireland,

child Autumn, Louise, Norris Born October 20,1998 Ireland, Katherine, Norris Born March16,1991 Ireland, Husband Stewart, Law Born October 03,1968 Ireland.

Father William, Lewis, Allen Born June 21,1935, married September22,1962 Ireland, Wife Catherine, Creswell Born November 26,193 died12 February 2012 Ireland,

Children Andrew, William, Allen Born June 29,1963 Ireland, Wife Decanis, Molloy, Shirleen, Catherine Allen Born July 04,1966, HusbenTony, Nauguhen, Denise, Margret Allen Born November 24,1967, Husband Adrain, Lord, Adrain, Sammy Born April 06,1973, Tony, James, Allen Born March 11,1975, Wife Wendy, Jasco, Grandchildren Niall Born1985 Ireland, Daniel, Born 1986 Ireland, James, Born 1988 Ireland, Zara, Born 1991Ireland, Alex, Born 1992 Ireland, Denise, Born 2000, Ireland, Christen, Born 20002Ireland, Sofia, Born20006 Ireland, James, Born 20008 Ireland,

Grate Grandchildren, Ternan, Born 20006 Ireland, Dylan, Born 20007 Ireland.

No 27. Charlie, Allen & Joyce Whitfield & Family

Charlie was born in Londonderry North Ireland, July 12, 1942.

Married Joyce Barbara Whitfield born September 18, 1942. They had 3 children.

Liam Charles Whitfield Allen born March 21, 1973, wife Helen Wakeboard April 19, 1972, child Nischa Eleanor Allen March 12, 1995,

Anninna Elizabeth Allen September 02,1960,

Angela Marie Allen January 24,1962. The two girls were Joyce from another marriage. Charlie raised them from little, and they took his last name, for he was like a real dad to them. Charlie was still in the army when they meet. He was with the Queens Royal Hussars, from the 23rd May, 1963 to 25 of April, 1972. As a civilian he drove for the army for a short time, he has been a factory worker, a H.G.V. Lorry driver a coal man and his job of 20 years working on the bus's in Swanage. After Liam was born, we moved into the next road (bigger) house, we were there 9 years. then we had the opportunity to move to Tall Trees, it was a derelict cottage that had a closing order declared inhabitable, the money we made from the sale of linden road give us the money to do the renovations, it has a acre of land the cottage was small, but the girls made their own way in the world. And it was just Liam and us. We put a caravan on the land and lived there till the house was done. We moved here, we decided to down size and have the money for our retirement. Joyce had 2 heart operations, she was on a life support machine for 10 days, the garden became a lot. Joyce early working life was hotel work and as a night nurse, In Swanage Hospital for 20 years. She said I loved it, now we are both retired. Charlie loved his running, he belongs to the local club and has run 3 London marathons and 1 in New York, and we belong to a walking group, a Dottie, me a heart club 60s club. We get out and about in the car and we enjoy our garden. Charlie and Joyce you are both grate people. And we are so glad you are in our family.

Memories of Charlie & Joyce Allen
By Them.

No 28. Bertie and Mabel Allen

Bertie Allen was the first born to Margaret and Robert Allen.

He had a good child hood; later on he had four other brothers'

And two sisters. They are very close to each other. Later on in his life he married

Two Mabel they had no children but enjoyed their other nieces and nephews.

We are glad you are in our family. By Evelyn Haywood Friend.

James Allen & Sarah Rabbit & Family

The Allen Family

James Allen was Born January 6, 1938 in Londonderry North Ireland, he lived there with his mother Margaret Gurney, and father Robert Allen along with his brothers, and sisters. They were a very close nit family. His wife Sarah who was referred to as Sally sum times she was born in September 1986. Later on in his life he did get married to Sarah Teresa Rabbit. They were married at Peck ham registry Office London. James was in the army in Germany. They lived on the base, that is where Sarah his wife had there to children, Christine Allen Born December 16, 1965. Jacqueline Born October 30, 1967. When in the arm fours, One does not know when they will be transferred out to a other place. It can be hard on the whole family, if the children are in school. I don't know about there, but here in Canada the children have to have high marks because every place and country is difference. They are to be excited to be in there 80's and 90's. Because sum places are high and others low in marking. The Schooling is a little difference on the bases, and the boys do ware white shirts and gray pants and blue blazers and ties. They had a dress code. I know that because my boys had to when we lived on base. James and Sarah have had a good life, and are retired now. We love you all and are glad you are in our family.

Memories of James Allen & Family
By Evelyn Friend,(Haywood)

Raymond, Allen & Ann Mcbride & Family

Donna, Raymond, Ann and Stephen Allen (2002)

Raymond Allen was Born April 11, 1944 he died on July 03 2003 of Cancer in the gullet, lived at 19 Pump Street Londonderry, with his family. He is buried in Ann's family grave at Killea(on the letterkenny road). He was a quite boy who loved his family. Sum of us didn't know you very well but from what we heard you were a very special person and we hope you are at peace now. He married in the chapel at Killea to Ann Mcbride on January 08, 1970. Ann was born May 04, 1945 in Killea co Donegal. Raymond worked at Gransha hospital maintenance the hospital. Raymond and Ann had three daughters.

Donna Allen Born October 23,1971 and she married Stephen Mattewson August 01,1971.

Bernadette Allen Born December 30,1973 and married Kenneth McGlinchey August 25,1973.

Katherine Allen Born November 23,1974, and she married Mark McBride Born April 01, 1974.

Bernadette and Katherine lives' near their mother Ann.

Donna lives in Scotland. Raymond and Ann were very close to the girls. Raymond and Ann and to your family, we are glad all of you are part of our family.

Memories of Raymond &Ann Allen.
By Evelyn Friend (Haywood)

Mary May Allen & Robert Norris & Family

Mary May Allen was Born February 05, 1937 in Londonderry North Ireland, May as she was called was a very quite girl, as she was growing up. She looks out for the others children and would help them from time to time. When I went to visit them all we all got a long and May and Lila and I hung out together been girls. We would go to all the dances. And to all other places like, Port Rush, you could ride horses there. We had so much fun together. Later on May meet William Norris Born May 24, 1937. They were married March 28, 1964. They had two children, Robert Norris Born September 21, 1965 in Londonderry North Ireland, on July 05, 1996 he married Caraline Bennet, Born June 24, 1962, child Autumn-Louise Born October 20, and 1998.

Katherine Norris Born April 27, 1967, she married Stewart Law March 16,1991, Stewart Law Born Oct.03,1968.

Robert Norris May's husband, they call him Willie. Is a very nice guy, who loves his children and of cores May is the love of his life. He had 2 strokes. He was in the hospital for a time, and May was there by his side. They came to Canada with their two children for a visit, we all had fun, I took the two kids with me and my kids to see a rock concern, Robert had never been to one. The guy said what you would like to hear. Of cores, Robert stayed Evils, he was yelling it out, I didn't know how much he loved him, till then. He was crazy for Evils. All his room had thing from Evils. He took back a clock with him. We had a hard time to get him on the plain again to go home. We told him if he still felt the same when he came of age he could come back. He was so not going back. We were worried for a while. It was so good to see them all. And Robert never came back so I guess he is happy where he is. May and Willie they are retired now, and just moved into a bungle. We all wish you and your family well. We are so glad you are in our family.

Memories of May & Willie Norris
By Evelyn Friend (Haywood)

Elizabeth, Lila, Allen & Michael Harrison & Family

Lila was born in Londonderry Northern Ireland in August, 19, 1939. She lived there with her family. Lila was a happy go lucky person. She has lovely brown curly hair, and a great smile. She also a proud person. She was always close with her family. Later on in her life she meets Michael Harrison, Born July 17, 1937. They did marry on February,23, 1957. They had to lovely boys, Stephen Born February, 21, 1960, and Paul Born June 17, 1961. Both boys Born in Rosyth Scotland. They were a happy family. When Lila takes about them you can tell that Michael was the love of her life, and she would change it. Before Christmas Michael had told Lila he was experiencing chest pain, she told him to get it checked out at the doctor. But he muffed it off, he probably though it was hart burn. They had a lovely Christmas with the family. The next day on the 26, of December, 2010 Lila found him in his chair. He had died very peafowl. It was a real shock for all the family. Lila would say he was a very livening and peaceful person, who loved his family. It's hard to lose a love one, but God had other plans for him. I am sure he is looking over them all. We love you Lila and Michael and your family, we are happy you are in our family.

Memory of Lila and Michael Harrison
By Evelyn Friend(Haywood)

William and Catherine Allen and Family.

Father William, Lewis Allen born 1935.
Wife Catherine, Creswell born 1936, died 2012.

Married 1962.

Child (1) Andrew, William, Allen born 1963.
Child(2) Denise, Margret, Allen born 1967.
Child (3) Adrain Sammy, Allen born 1973.
Child(4) Tony, James, Allen born 1975.
Child(5) Deirdre, Molloy, Shirleen, Allen born 1966.

No 34. Evelyn Gurney, & Charlie Sherratt & Family.

Evelyn Gurney was born May 03, 1921, in Londonderry North Ireland; she lived there with her Mother Sarah Wallace, and Father William Gurney, and brothers and sisters. When she got older, she thought she would like to live in Canada with her sister Mary and Brother Lewis but when she got there she didn't like it, maybe it was too much of a difference in the size and paste. She did return back to Ireland. Well it was just as well for Evelyn would have not meet Charles, Harold, William, Sherratt. Charles was a petty Office in the Navy, who was Born December 25, 1918, who was from England. He was a very Hanson man, and so well groomed, and polite, and well mannered, and the nicest smile who would like him. I know when I went over there with my mother we stared at their place, and he made sure that we had a good time. But at the same time were safe. Before my cousins May and Lila and myself Evelyn, went off, he had a little take with us. (He said now girls, on every ship there is two list, one for the good girls and one for the bad ones, and I do not want to see any of your names on either, we said know uncle Charlie.) He is a real sweet and caring man. He came to Canada for a visit with his son Dereck. We had a real good time, we went for a walk one day and we came across a bee nest, so Dereck picked, up Rose-Anna our youngest and we all run. That happens when one lives in the country. When my Mother and dad were living, he did a picture in needle point for them, of a ship, and my mother got it framed, before she died she gave it to me, and it is hanging in my living room today, It will always be in the family I was sorry to hear that Uncle Charlie had a bad few months with colon cancer plus a mild stroke. He is a very special person. Evelyn and Charlie did marry, February 14,1942, in Londonderry North Ireland. They tried to have children, but they though they couldn't, so they adopted a sweet little girl, and named her Carole, Evelyn, Isobel, Ann, Sherratt. Born February 07, 1949, they were over joined with her. She had red hair and so sweet. After a while Carole, had become part of their family, Aunt Evelyn had a little girl to their surprise, which they named Hester Grace. Born August 14, 1942. And of cores they were so happy for they had two little girls. A few years past and she had a little boy; they named him Dereck, Charles, Sherratt. Born May 18, 1957, now they really felt blessed, from thinking they couldn't have any children to having three children. A few years later they decided to move to Scotland, and were very happy there, then Aunt Evelyn took sick and died, of Myocardial inxavetion, on October 1984. She had gone to rest in her bed, and after a while he went up stairs and found her. She had passed away in her sleep. Charlie cared very deeply for her and made sure he looked after her. Charlie was still living in Scotland in his home with care, his health declined this past year Hester and her daughter Kim visited in March and was in great form and thoroughly enjoyed seeing the Great Grandchildren. Carole and Hester visited regularly. And his son Dereck has been a good son and wife Sandra. His death came as a shock, he was 93 years old in April 2011. We will remember him with a smile as he all way's looked on the positive of life.

Carole married Robert Brankley March 25, 1972.

Children Nicola Born August 05, 1978, Christopher Born January 25, 1983. Nicola married Peter Wilton Jones, July 29, 2007

Hester Grace married William, (Ivan) John, Graham. March 29, 1980.

Children Kim was born July 04, 1983, Dale Born April 12, 1990.

Kim married Peter Martin Knox, September.10, 2005,

Children Ellie Grace Born September 06,2006, Max Peter Born March 28,2007.

Dereck, Charlie, married Sandra Workman September 27,1986.

Children Daniel Born November 11, 1987. Beverley Born February 10, 1990.

I am sure there are a lot of more stories that could be tolled of this family. We are so very glad that all of you are part of our family. Memory's of Charlie and Evelyn Sherratt

By Evelyn Friend(HAYWOOD)

No 34. The Names and Dates OF Sherratt Family's.

(1,) Father Charles, Harold, William, Sherratt, Born December 25,1918 England, Died April 05,2011 Scotland, Wife Evelyn, Gurney, Born May 03,1921, Londonderry Ireland, married February 14,1942, Died October 15, 1984 Scotland, Children 1, Carole, Evelyn, Isobel, Ann, Sherratt, Born Febuary07,1949 Londonderry, Ireland, 2, Hester, Grace, Sherratt, Born August 14, 1950, Londonderry, Ireland, 3, Dereck, Charles, Sherratt, Born May 18, 1957, Londonderry, Ireland.

(2,) Father Robert, Brankley Born Ireland, married March25, 1972 Wife Carole, Evelyn, Isobel, Ann, Sherratt, Born February 07, 1949 Londonderry, Ireland, Children 1, Nicola, Brankley, Born August 05, 1978 Ireland, Nicola married Peter, Wilton, Jones, July 29, 2007 Ireland 2, Christopher, Brankley, Born January 25, 1983 Ireland.

(3,) Father Ivan, John, Graham Born Ireland, married March29, 1980, Wife Hester Grace, Sherratt, Born August 14, 1950 Londonderry, Ireland, Children 1, Kim, Graham, Born July 04, 1983 Ireland,2, Dale, Graham, Born April 12, 1990 Ireland.

(4,) Father Peter, Martin, Knox, Born Ireland married September10, 2005 Ireland, Wife Kim, Graham Born July 04, 1983 Ireland, Children 1, Ellie, Grace, Knox Born September 06, 2006 Ireland,2, Max, Peter, Knox, Born March 28,2007 Ireland.

(5,) Father Dereck, Charles, Sherratt, Born May18,1957 Londonderry, Ireland, Wife Sandra, Workman, married September 27,1986 Ireland, Children 1, Daniel, Sherratt, Born November 11,1987 Ireland,2, Beverley, Sherratt, Born Febuary10,1990 Ireland.

Lewis Gurney

Lewis Gurney arrived at Quebec City (1929)

Lewis Gurney born August 5,1914, died August 29,1980. Lila, Grace, Grinney born January 29,1921 married December 20,1941 died July 10,1987. Theyhad Four Children, Nancy, Louise, Gurney, Sharon, Lee, Gurney, Sandra, Lynn, Gurney, & Wallace, Scott, Gurney. Each one Married and had children, they also have grand children, and they have a big family, and are very close. I know their children were raised on a farm, which their parents bout. Their mother and dad worked very hard, aunt Lila was a favourite aunt she would say come on now and give you a big smile, she was happy working outside, and could work along with any man. She also had a big garden and was a good cook and baker. Uncle Lewis was loved by all two. He came to Canada when he was a young boy from Londonderry Ireland; he was put on a farm to work his passage off that was the way a lot came here at that time. After working for others, they saved engulf to buy their own farm. He loved his farm and worked hard along with his wife Lila they did a lot together. Their daughter Nancy did not want to live on a farm after she got married. But had a good life with her husband Robert Hulley and four children. Sharon on the other hand did live on a farm, with her husband Thomas Bickell and their three boys. Sandra did not, but is happy with her husband John Squire and their three boys. Wallace Gurney was a baker and had his own business also served in the army did marry but it did not work out that happens sum times. Their four children were their pride and joy a long with their grand children. I am sure there are many more stories's to be told. All of their family's are with this right up. We Love you all and are glad all of you are in our family.

William Lewis Allen

William was born November 22, 1935 in Londonderry North Ireland to Robert and Margaret Allen. He had a brother at the time, he was the second child at the time. Later on the family grew and there was seven in all. William was a very caring person who loves his family, and his extended family. Which he had lots. They are a close nit group. Later on he meet Catherine Creswell born November 26, 1936. Died 12 February 2012. The same year I am. They married September 22, 1962, and had five children, 9 grandkids, and 2 grates. They had sons and daughters. Niall William Allen born 1985, Daniel Allen lord born 1986, James Glyn Lord born 1988, Zara Shirleen Lord born 1991, Alex Malcolm Lord born 1992, Denise Allen born 2000, Christin Anthony Naughton Allen born 2002, Sofia Elizabeth Allen 2006, James Vacs Allen born 2008. The greats are McHenry Lord born 15, and Dylan Glen Lord born 10, April 2007. Son Andrew Allen wife is Deirdre Molloy, Shirleen Allen is my daughter, Adrain Sammy is also a son born 1973 he was married for 10 years. But it did not work out, no children. He is a lawyer livening in Indiana, U.S.A. Tony James Allen is also my son, then there is Denise Margret Allen my other daughter. I hope I got them all, they may not be in order. But I tried. You have a lovely family William & Catherine. Big families are nice. And we are glad you are a part of ours.

Memories by William & Catherine Allen.
By Evelyn Friend (Haywood).

No 24. William Gurney.

William Gurney was born in Londonderry North Ireland, in 1872.

He was a kind, loving, grandfather who loved his family; His father was James, Gurney and mother was Mary. William was a tall big man. When he was young he joined up in the army and went to war. And while he was fighting there was a lot going on around him, and at one point he was buried for three days alive, but he serviced. William liked to play the horses and gramma would get mad at him, but he never worried about that. William was a baker by trade, and a good one. That is why we are good cooks and baker we take after him. William was so happy when he heard that Mary Minnie Gurney his daughter and her daughter Evelyn were coming for a visit, but in the mean while he had a fell down and broke his hip. He was in hospital when we arrived, but he was so happy to see us. He said to me we are going to have a big party for you when I get out. But in those days they didn't know as much as they know today, and infection set in and he died. It was a sad day for all of us. I was looking forward to spending time with him and getting to know him more. In Ireland in those days the casket was in the house, and the men walked and woman rode. Mary his daughter and Evelyn said we would walk to the grave site. They did have a party, but he was there in spirit. He dies in July 16th, 1952. He married in December 25, 1900, to Sarah Wallace. We all love and miss you,

And are so glad you are in our family. May you rest in peace?

Memories of William Gurney.
By Evelyn Friend (Haywood) Granddaughter.

Lewis & Lila Gurney Family Tree				
	Born	**Married**	**Died**	
Lewis Gurney	8/5/1914		08/29/1980	
Lila Grace (Grinney) Gurney	01/28/1921		7/10/1987	John Victor Grinney 03/13/1892,10//11/1916, 1967.
		12/20/1941		Mary Jane Scott ,1896, 1950
				Jean Victoria Ginney 1923, 1980
***# 1 Nancy** Louise (Gurney) Hulley*	10/14/1942			James Victor Grinney Born03/13/1892.
Robert John Hulley	03/17/1941		01/30/2005	Lila Grace Grinney Born 08/28/1921, Died 7/10/1987.
		8/7/1961		
Tracy Louise (Hulley) Huxley*	12/18/1961			
Graham Huxley	11/17/1961			
		10/1/1981		Final This one
Bryan Frederick Stiefel*	7/9/1977			
Christine Anne McLaren	9/6/1981			
		not married		
Nolan Christopher Stiefel	07/16/2008			
Craig Allan Huxley	2/5/1981			
Jennifer Elizabeth (Anthony) Huxley	01/17/1982			
		09/22/2007		

Trystan-lyn Huxley	11/30/2008			
Tara Leanne Huxley	04/15/1983			
Bryan Joseph Scales	10/26/2002			
		not married		
Robert **Todd** Hulley	07/31/1964			
Cindy Harmsworth (divorced)*	02/25/1965			
		9/8/1986		
Denise Patricia (Mayville) Hulley	03/29/1968			
		06/25/2005		
Brittony Lynn Hulley*	05/28/1994			
Brianna Lee Hulley*	7/4/1996			
Jesse Robert Hulley*	09/29/1997			
Troy Darren Hulley	8/8/1966			
Dianne ( ) Hulley (divorced)*				
Lynne Hulley (Bechard)		06/30/2001		
Darren Robert Guy Hulley*	3/3/1989			
Ashley Dianna Louise Hulley*	08/17/1990			
Victoria Louise Hulley	12/17/2002			

Kevin Jameson Lewis Hulley	06/16/2004			
Tanya LeeAnn (Hulley) Van Dyk	08/25/1970			
Robert Van Dyk	9/11/1967			
		02/17/1995		
Tatiauna Mia Van Dyk	9/3/1997			
Nicholas Kynan Van Dyk	7/3/1998			
# 2 Sharon *Lee (Gurney) Bickell*	04/18/1946			
Thomas Kinsman Bickell	07/18/1936			
		9/12/1966		
Thomas **Wade** Bickell	6/8/1968			
Christina Nancy **(Tina)** (Marriott)	03/24/1968			
		07/29/1989		
Thomas **Ryan** Bickell	08/25/1999			
Cassandra Nancy Bickell	7/9/2003			
Jason Lewis Bickell	4/3/1970			
Teresa (Knapton) Bickell (divorced)	2/10/1966			
		8/10/1994		
Kyle Thomas Bickell	4/6/1996			
Emma Lynn Bickell	03/19/1998			

Joseph Michael Bickell	01/22/2002			
William Kyle Bickell	5/6/1977			
Shannon Adel Rice *	3/8/1971			
Connor Drew Rice *	07/18/1996			
Levi Ian Rice *	1/1/1999			
Evan William Rice *	8/5/2001			
***# 3 Sandra** Lynn (Gurney) Squire*	05/26/1953			
John Samuel Squire	11/5/1951			
		07/28/1972		
John Samuel Squire	3/12/1972			
Lisa Anne (Moyer) Squire	2/3/1974			
		05/16/1998		
Jacob Samuel Squire	09/15/1997			
Grace Mary Squire	7/6/2000			
William **Jason** Squire	06/28/1975			
Sarah Ann (Harrison) Squire	05/14/1975			
		04/26/2003		
Alexis Michelle Long Squire	7/9/1995			
William **Michael** Squire	6/11/2002			

James Thomas Squire	08/23/1977	9/16/2006		
Lisa Ellen (Lemon) Squire	4/12/1979			
Samuel James Squire	11/17/2010			
Jackson Walter Thomas Squire	4/3/2009			
# 4 Wallace ***Scott*** *Gurney*	04/29/1962			
Deborah (Wylie) Gurney	04/18/1962			
		7/9/1984		

FAMILY TREES

ALLEN-CRESWELL

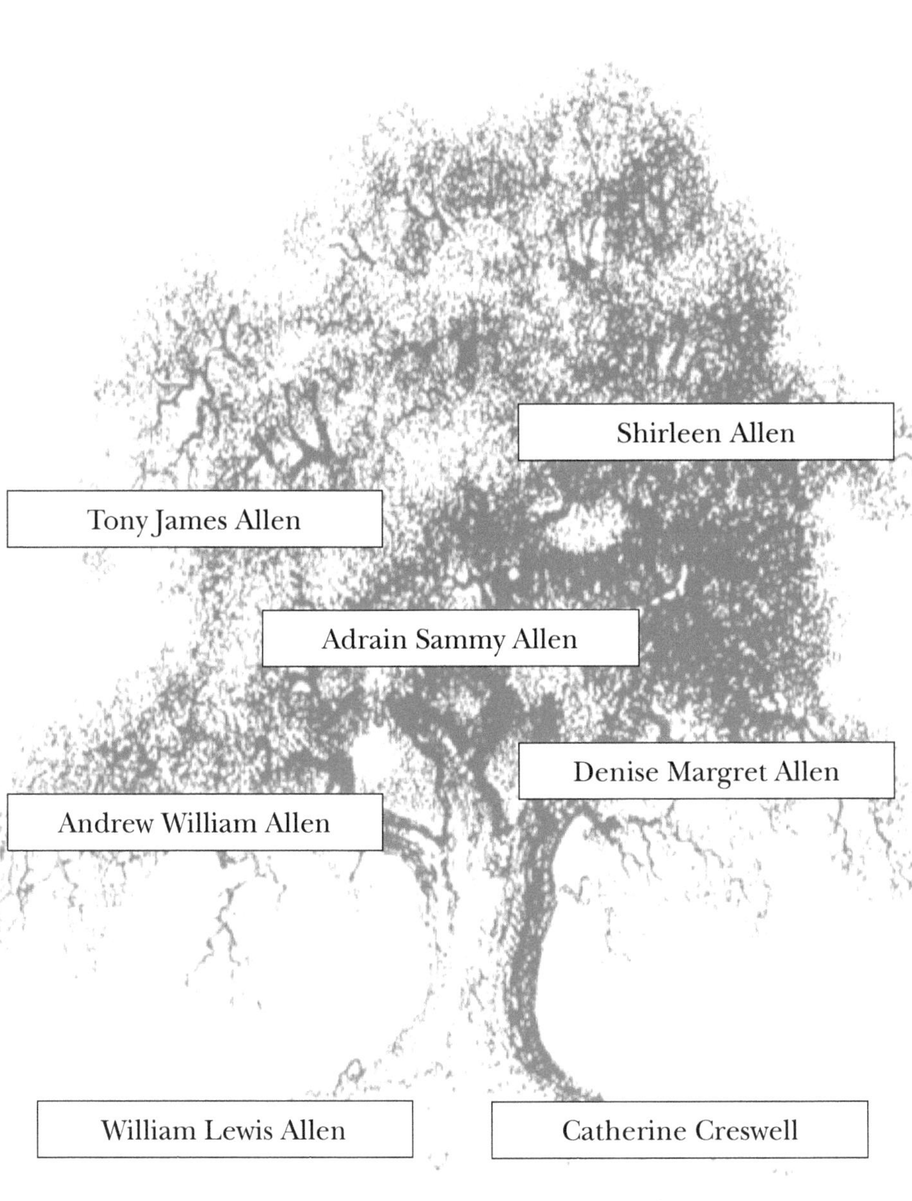

ALLEN-GURNEY

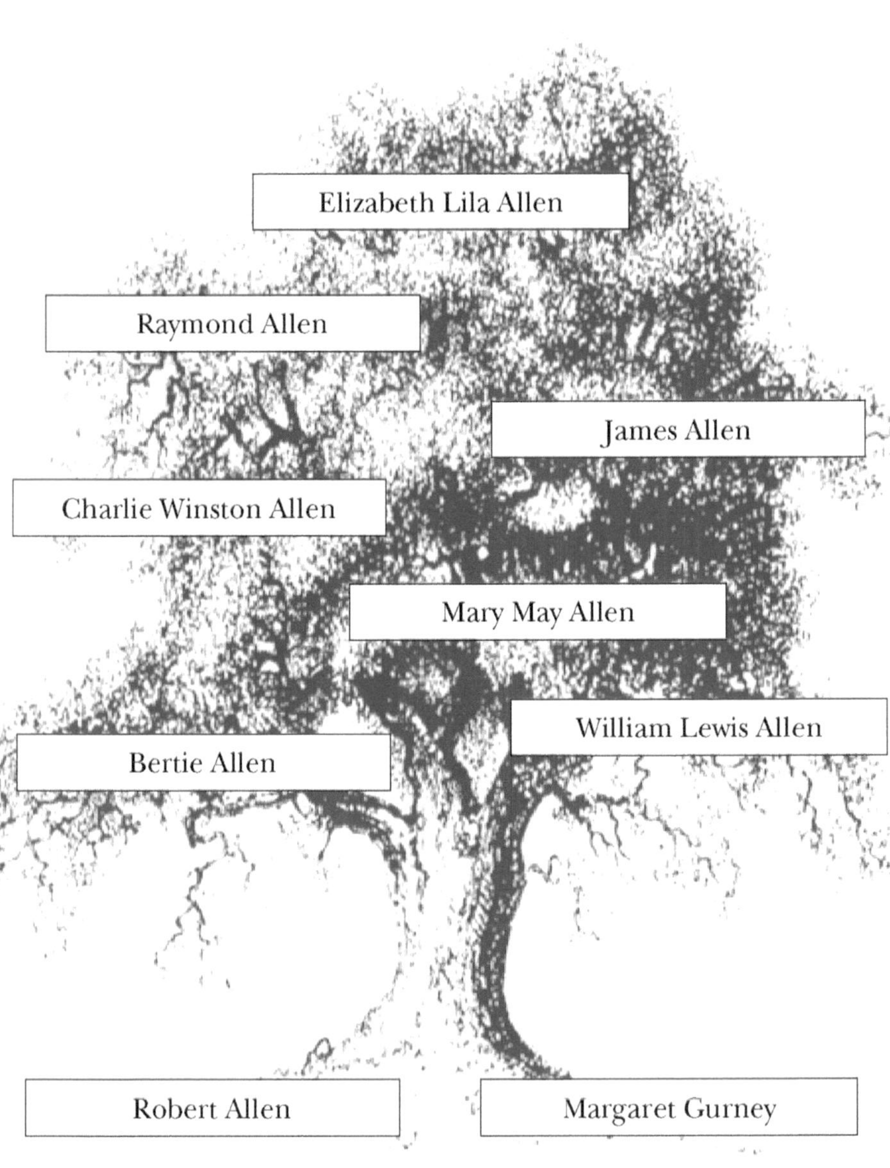

ALLEN-MCBRIDE

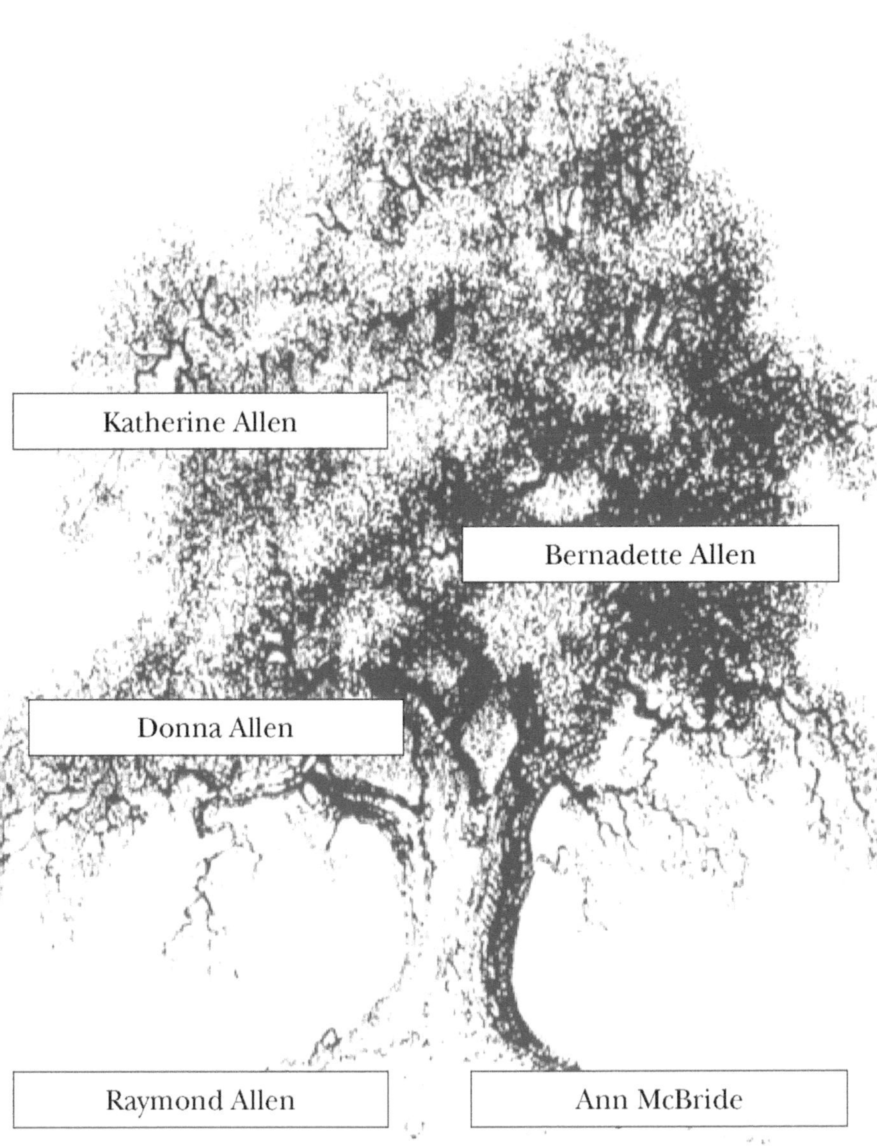

ALLEN-RABBIT

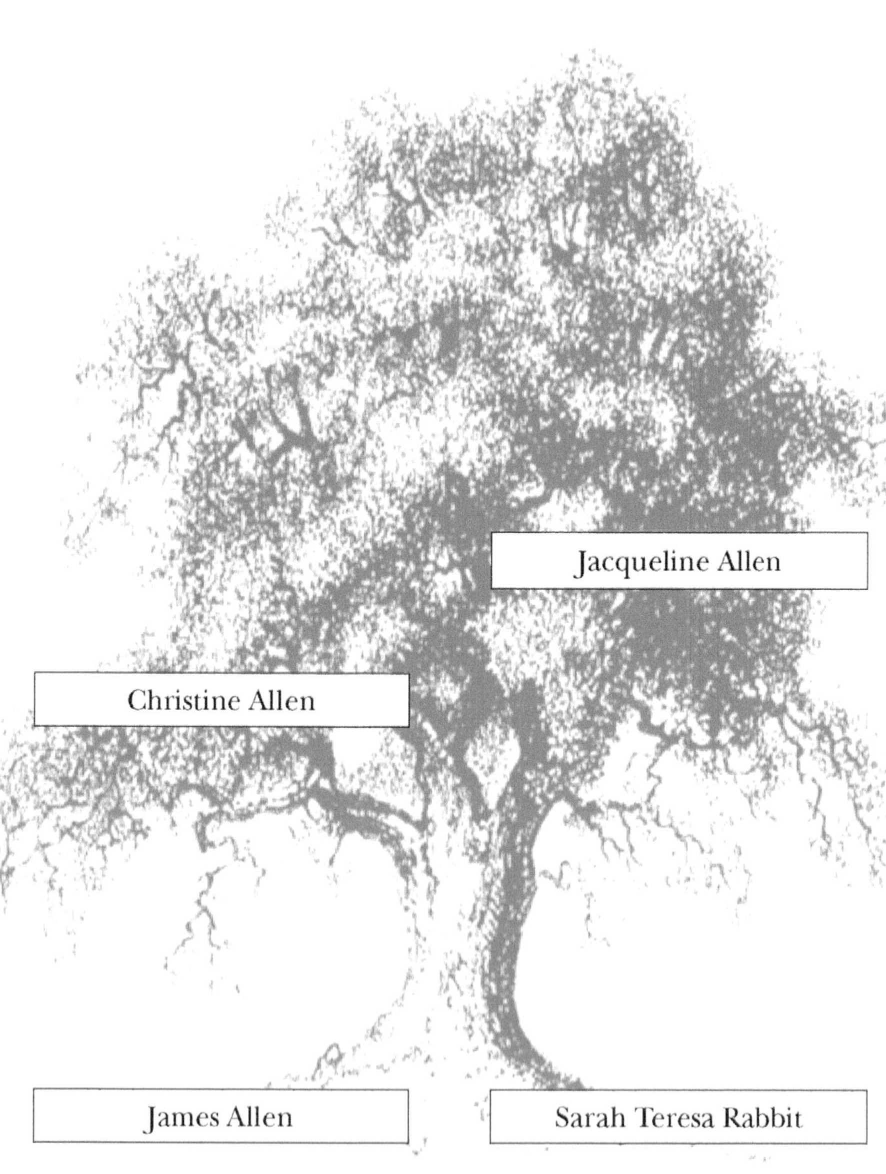

ALLEN-WHITEFIELD

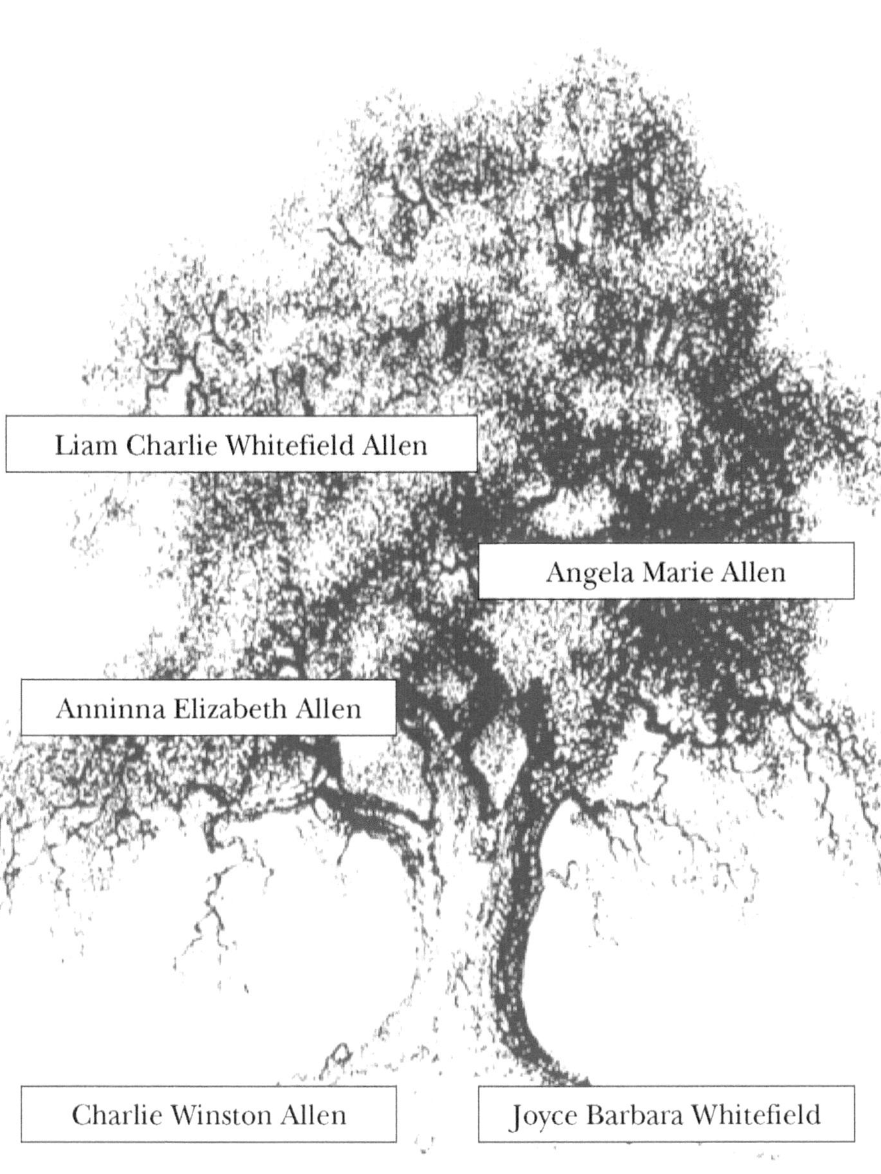

BICKELL-KNAPTON

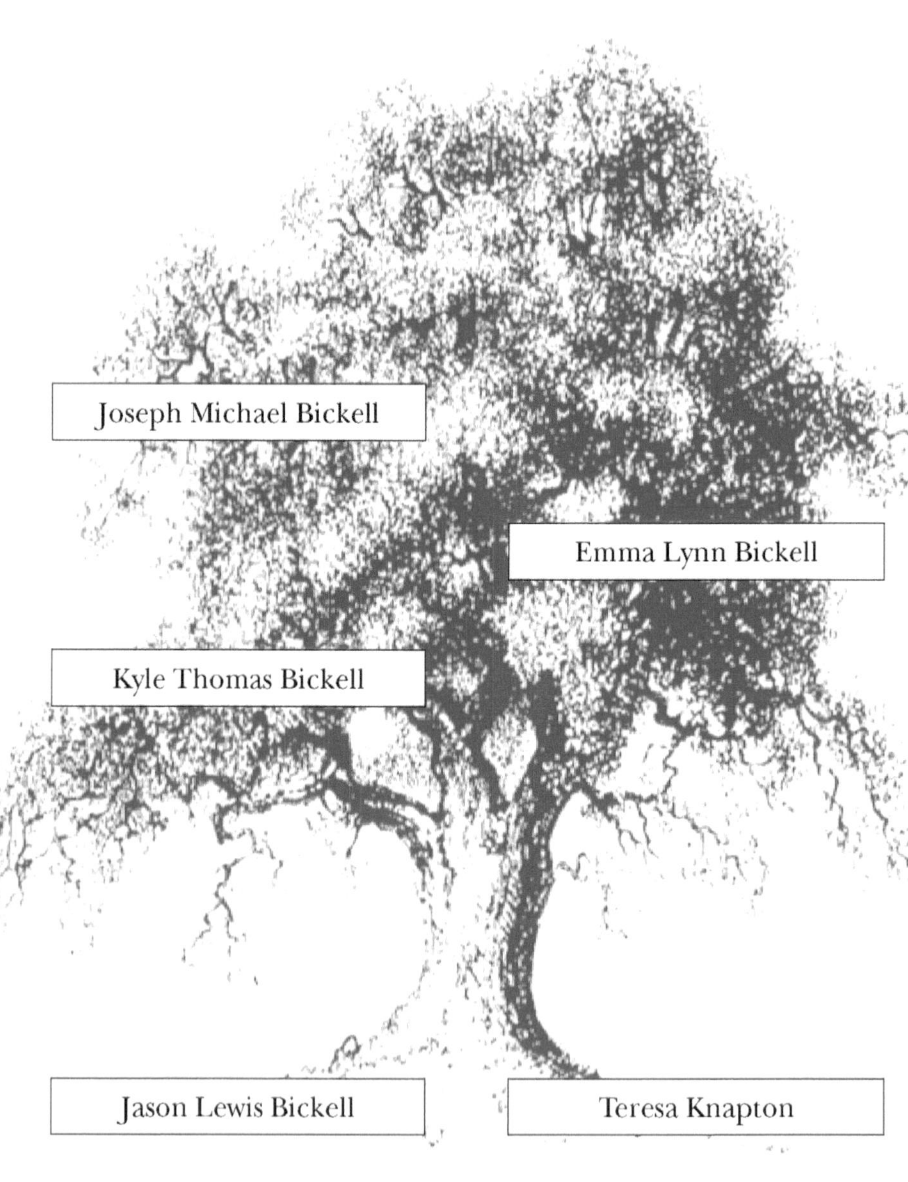

BICKELL-MARRIOTT

BICKELL-RICE

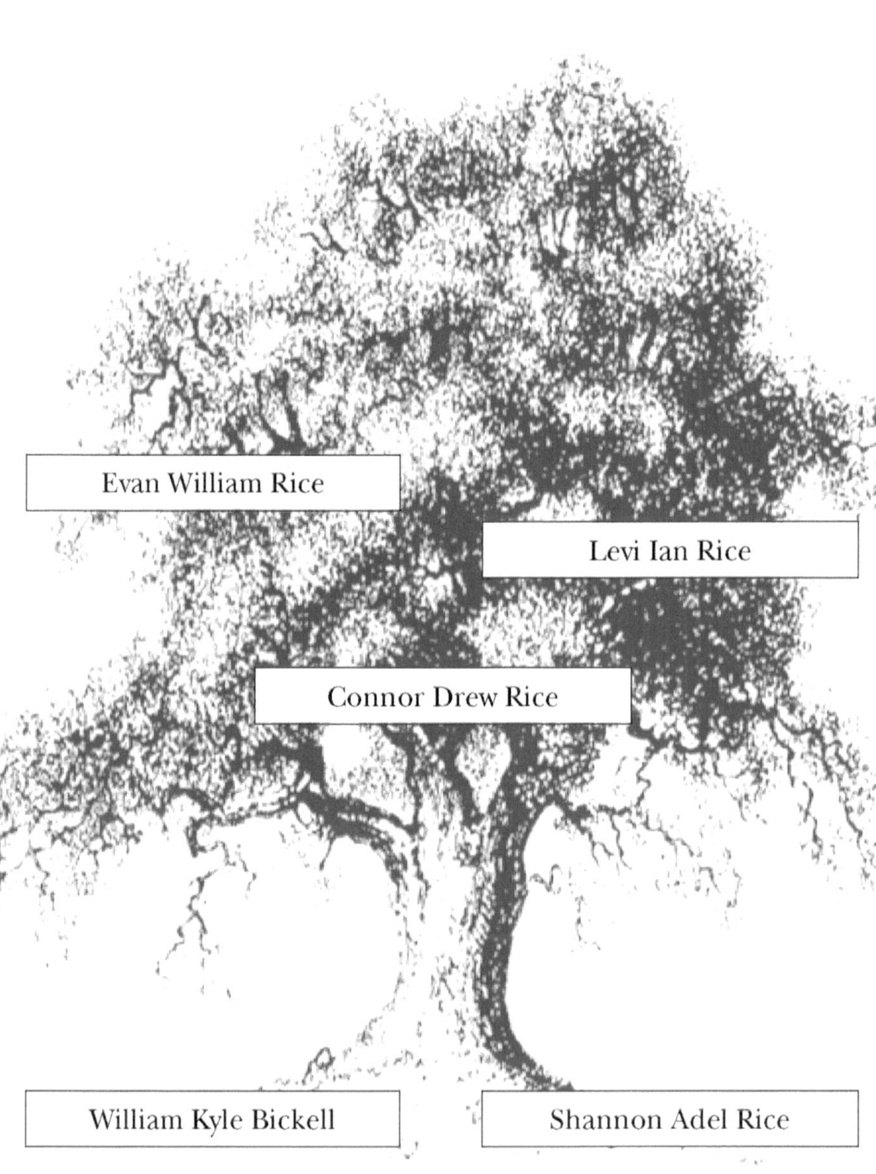

BRANKLEY-SHERRATT

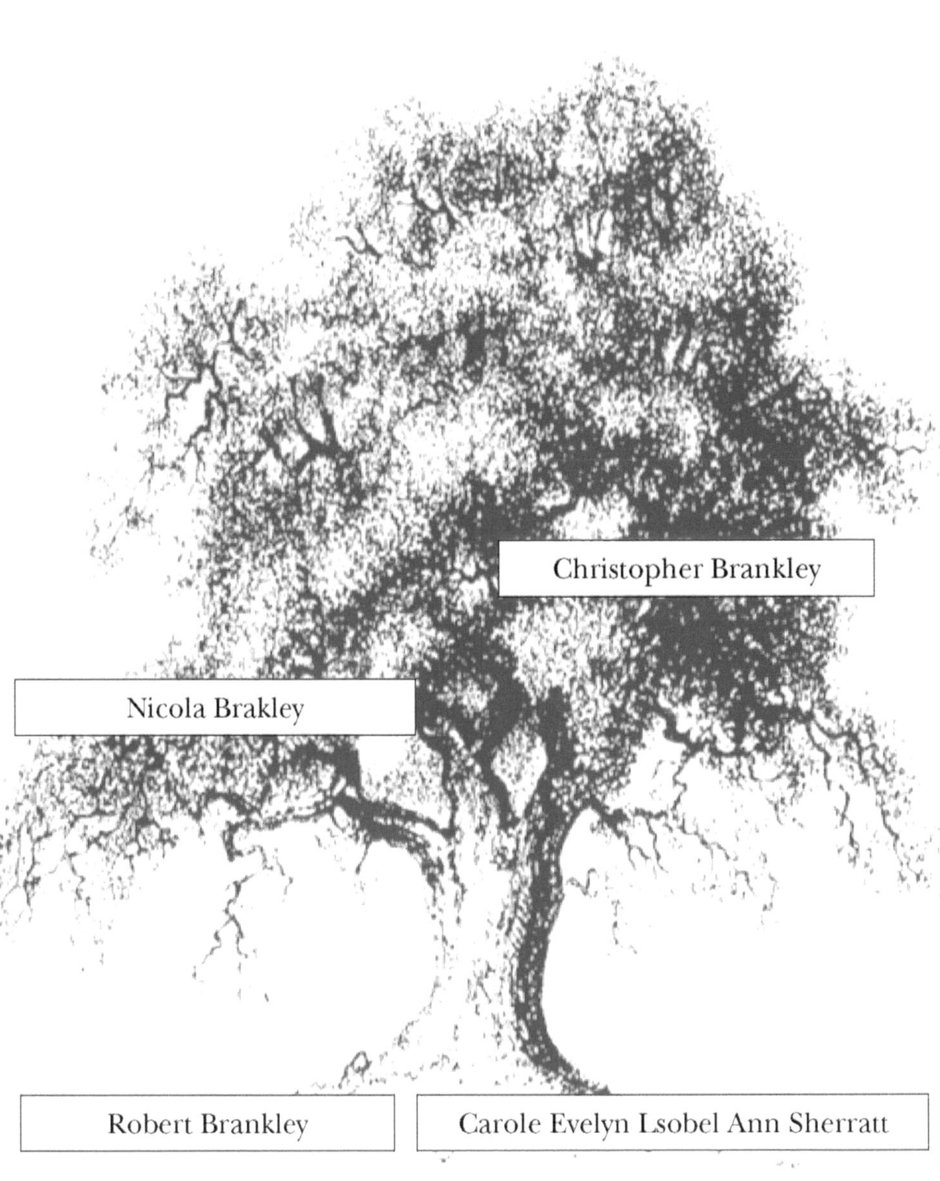

CARR-MARGARET

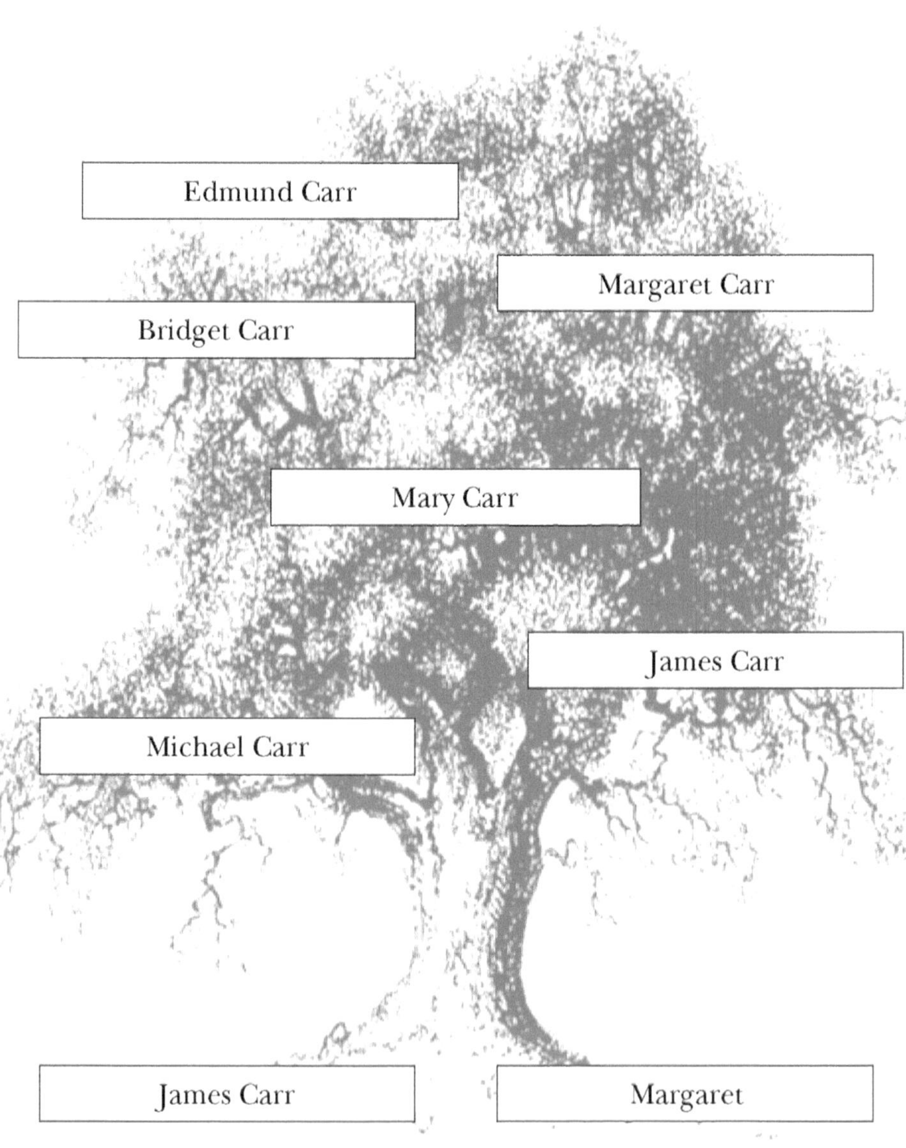

COLLETTE-SIMPSON

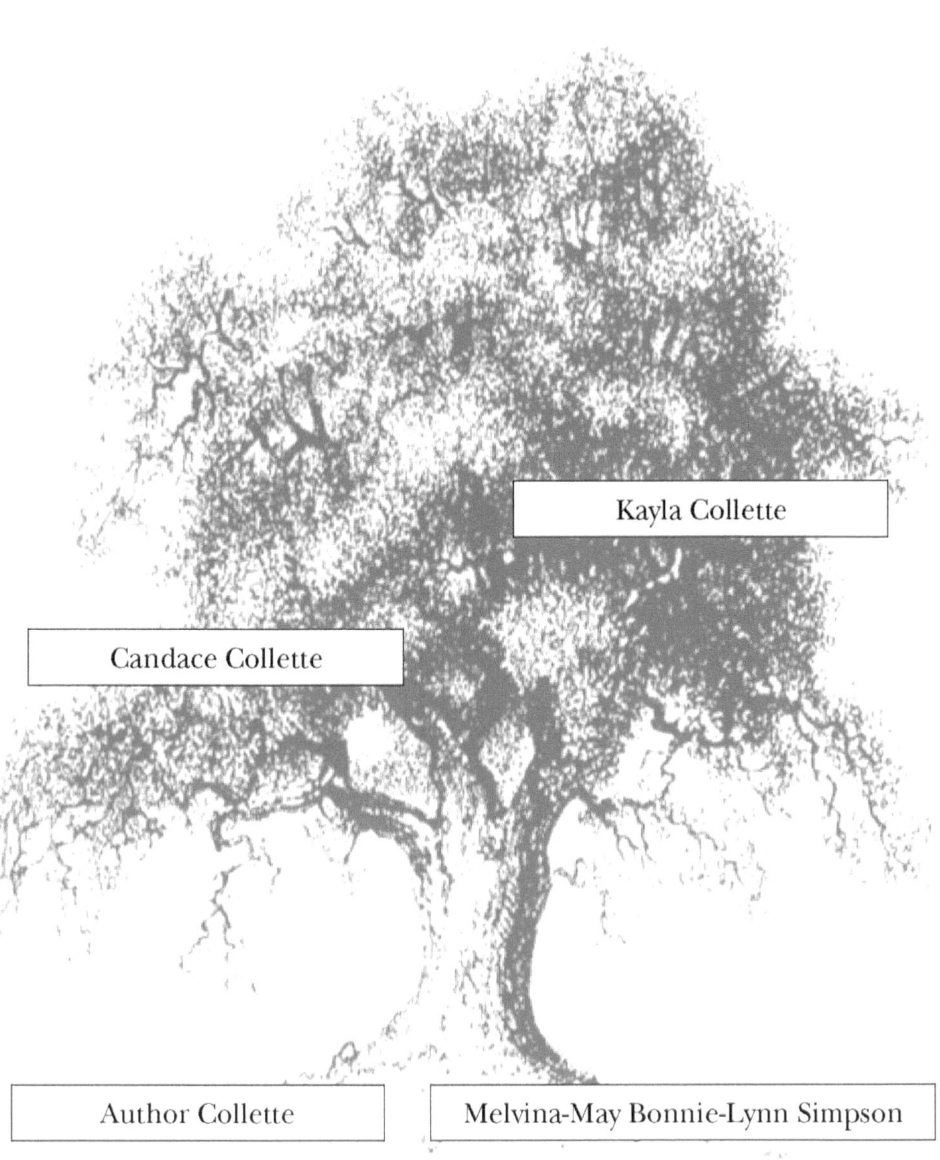

FRIEND-HAYWOOD-HOLMAN

FRIEND-HOLMAN

FRIEND-LAGGETT

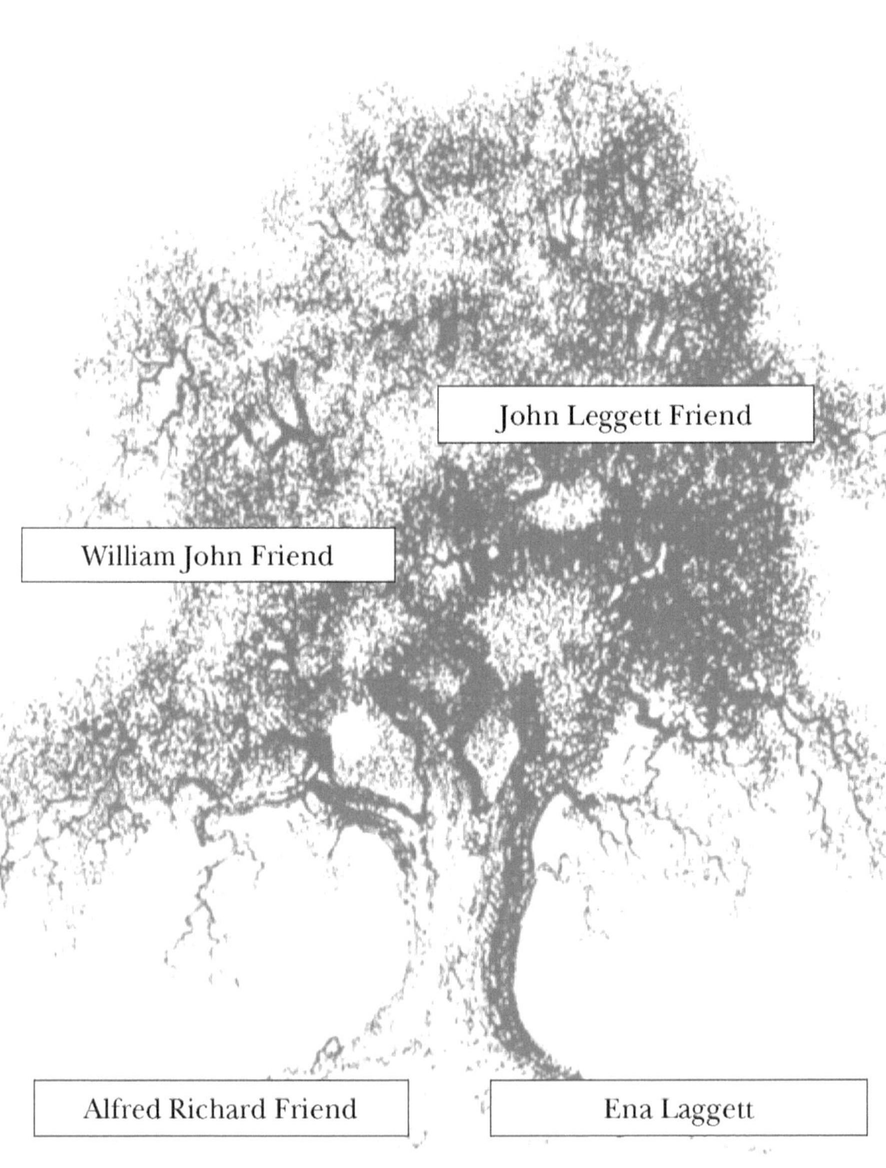

GRAHAM-SHERRATT

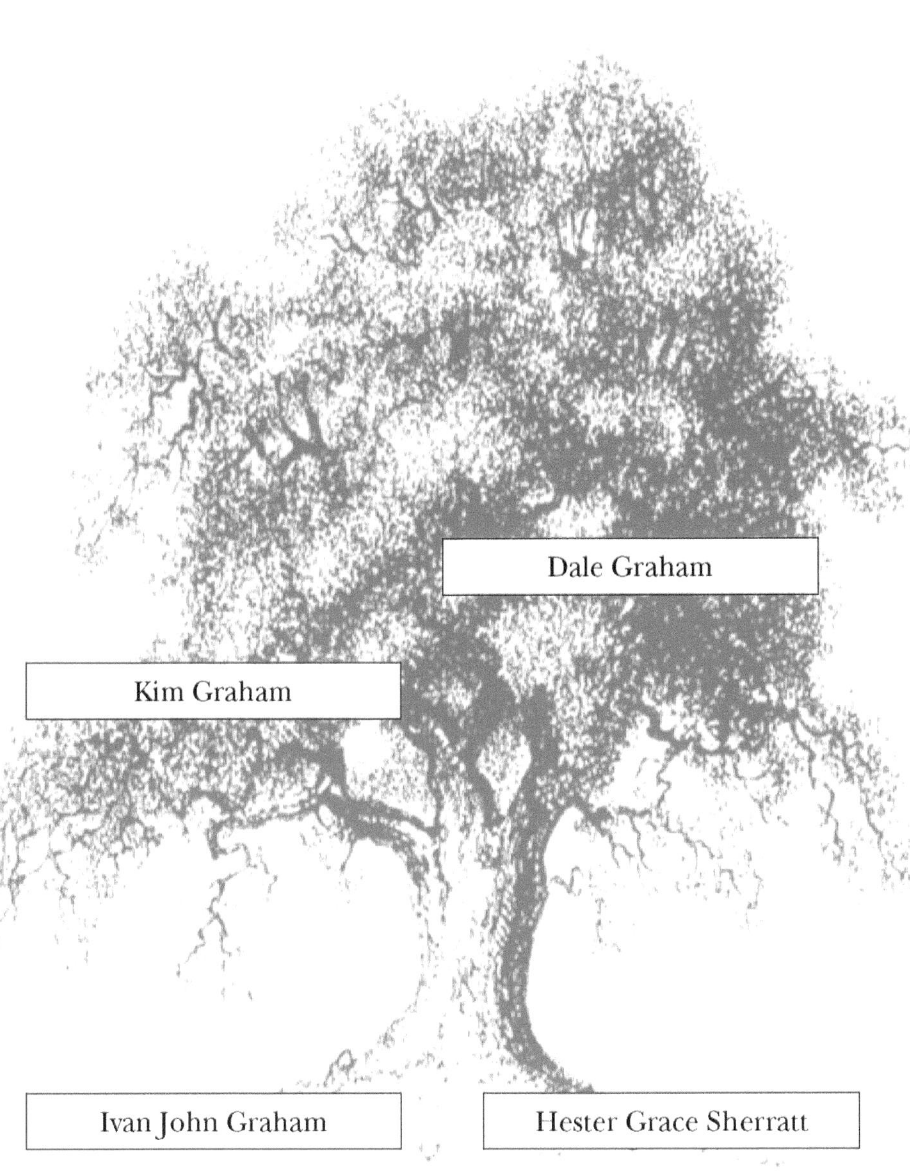

GROSS-TURKEY

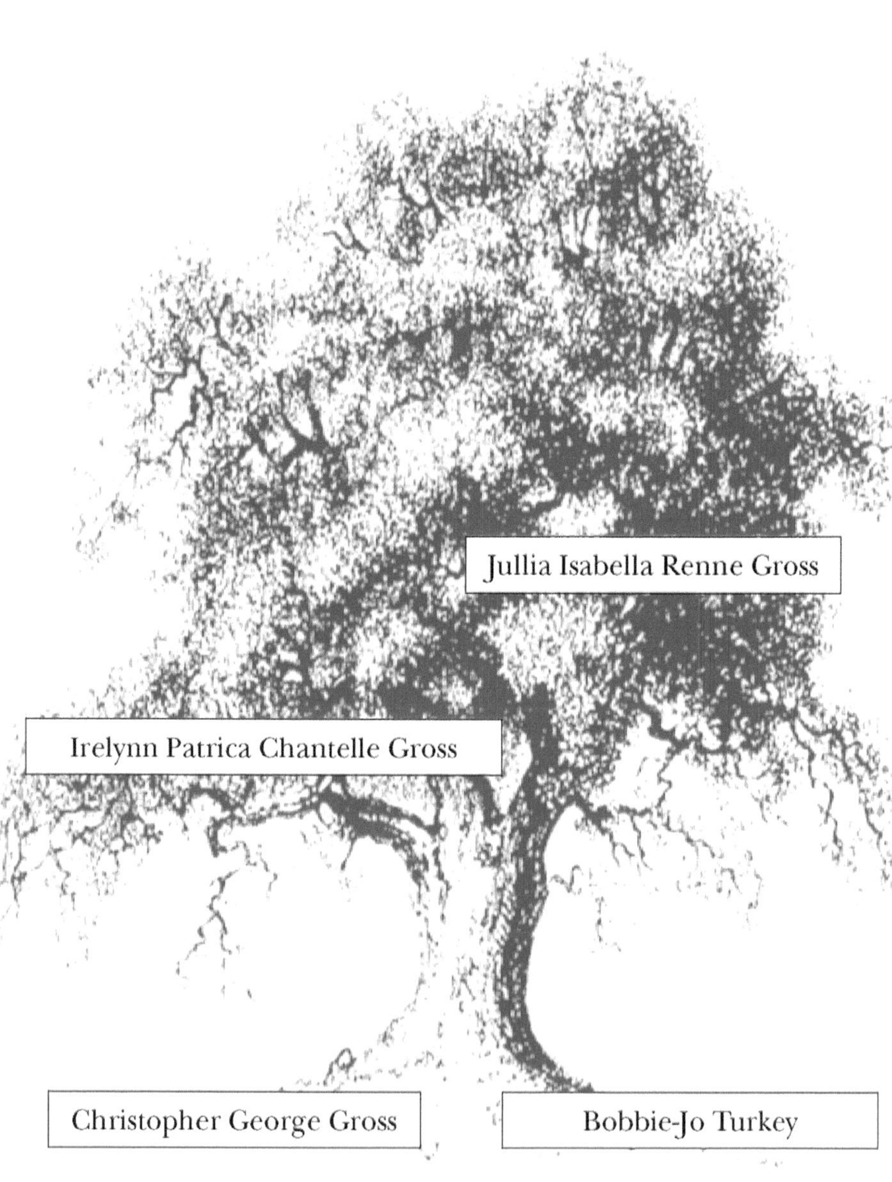

GURNEY-GRINNEY

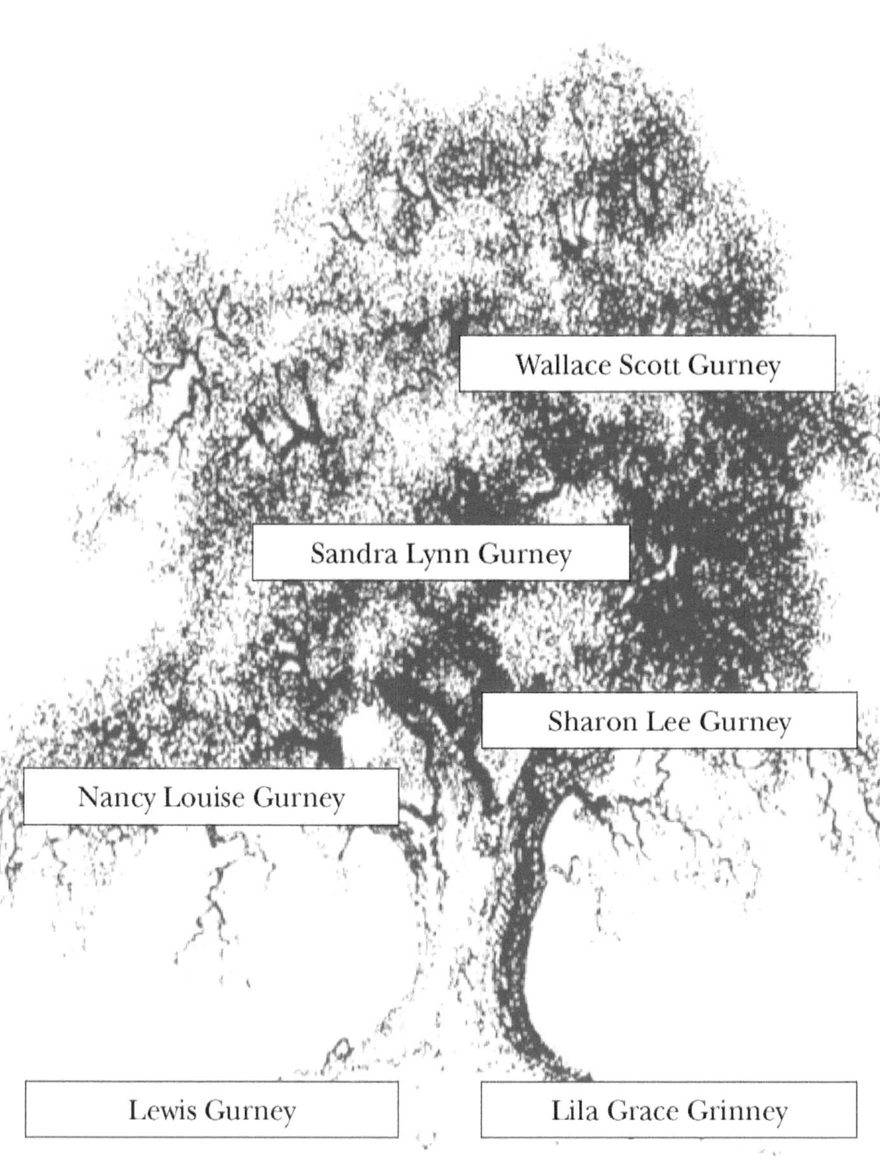

GURNEY-MARY

John Gurney
William Gurney
Mary Gurney
Jane Gurney
Maggie Gurney
James Gurney
Hugh Gurney
James Gurney
Mary

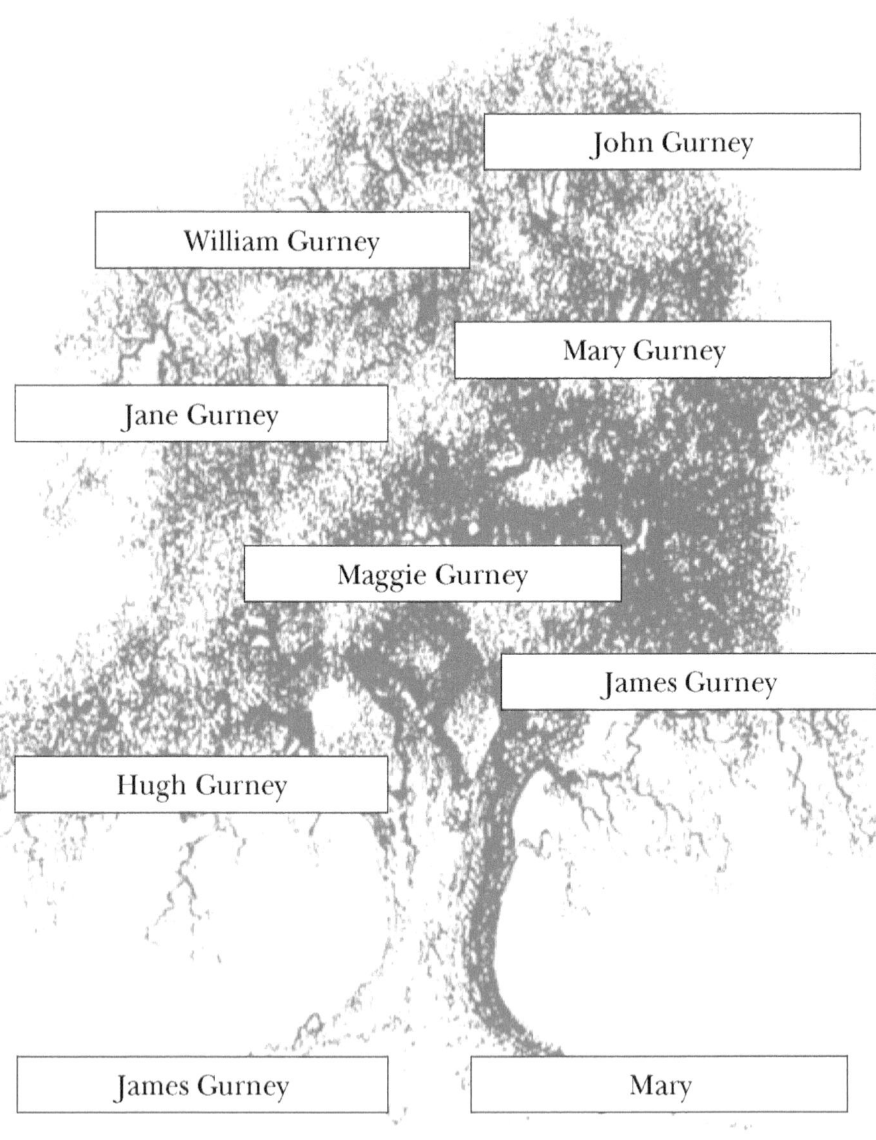

GURNEY-WALLACE

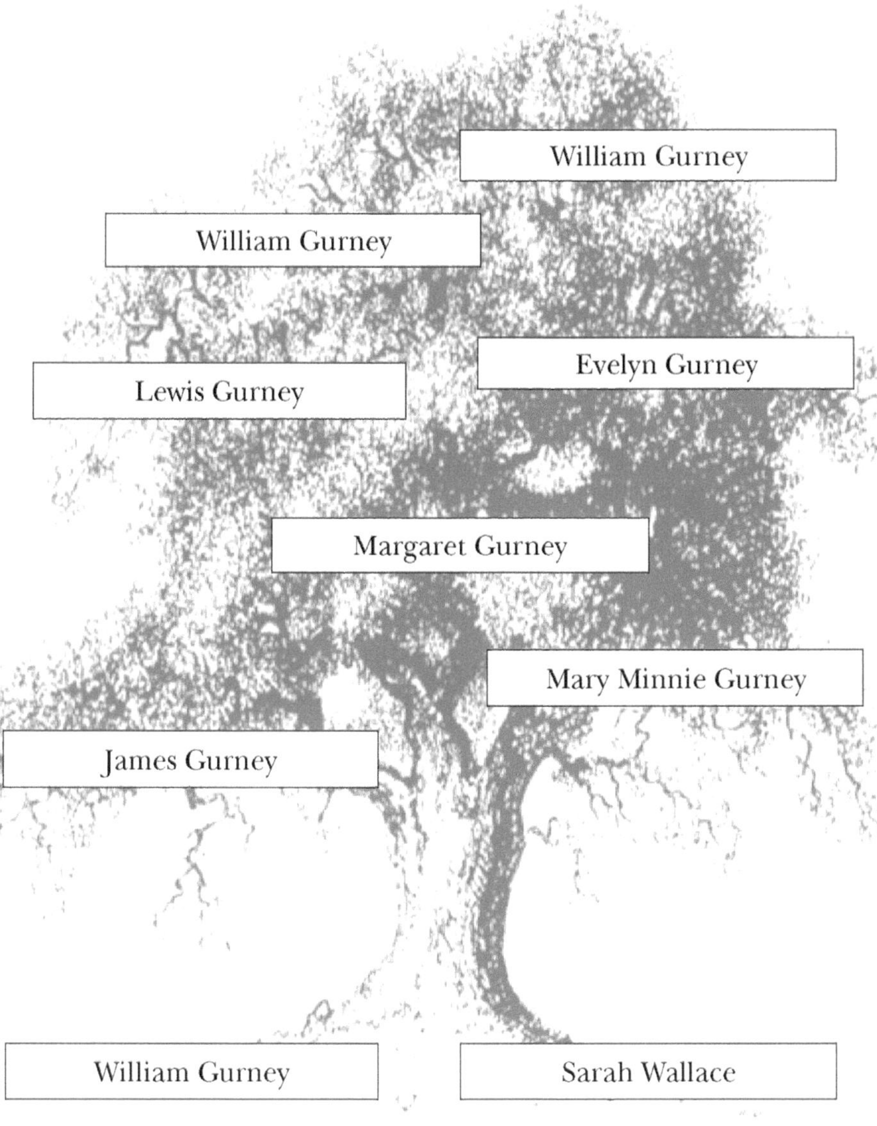

HARRISON-ALLEN

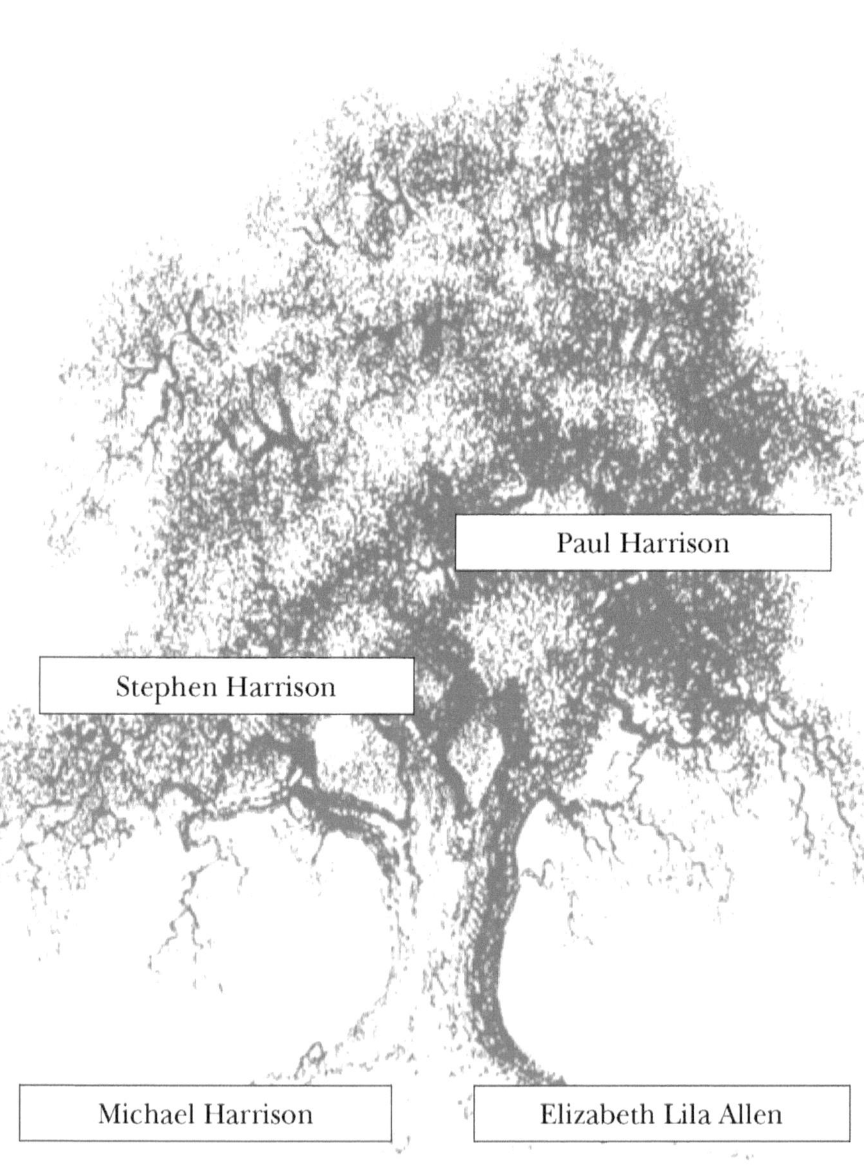

HAYWOOD-DARRAUGH

HAYWOOD-GARNETT

HAYWOOD-ROBERTS

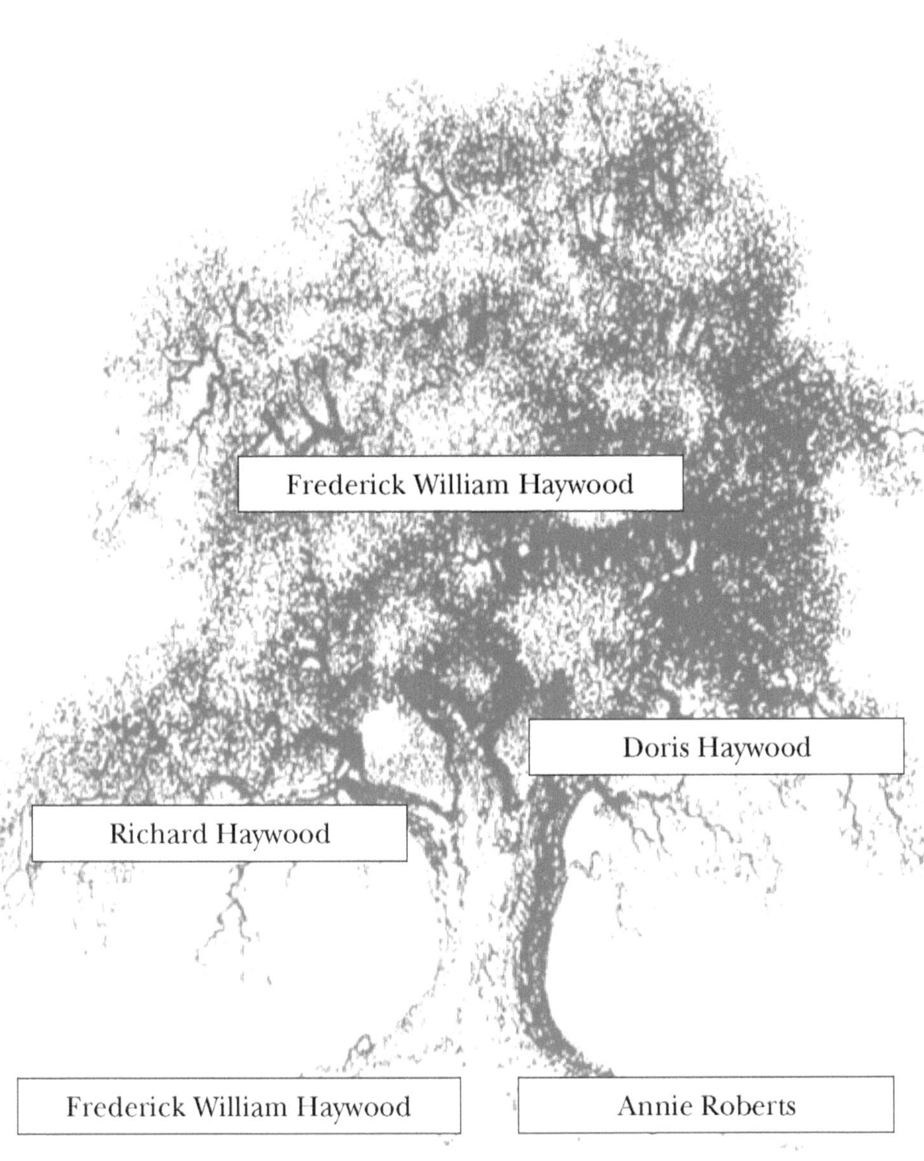

HAYWOOD-SNELLING

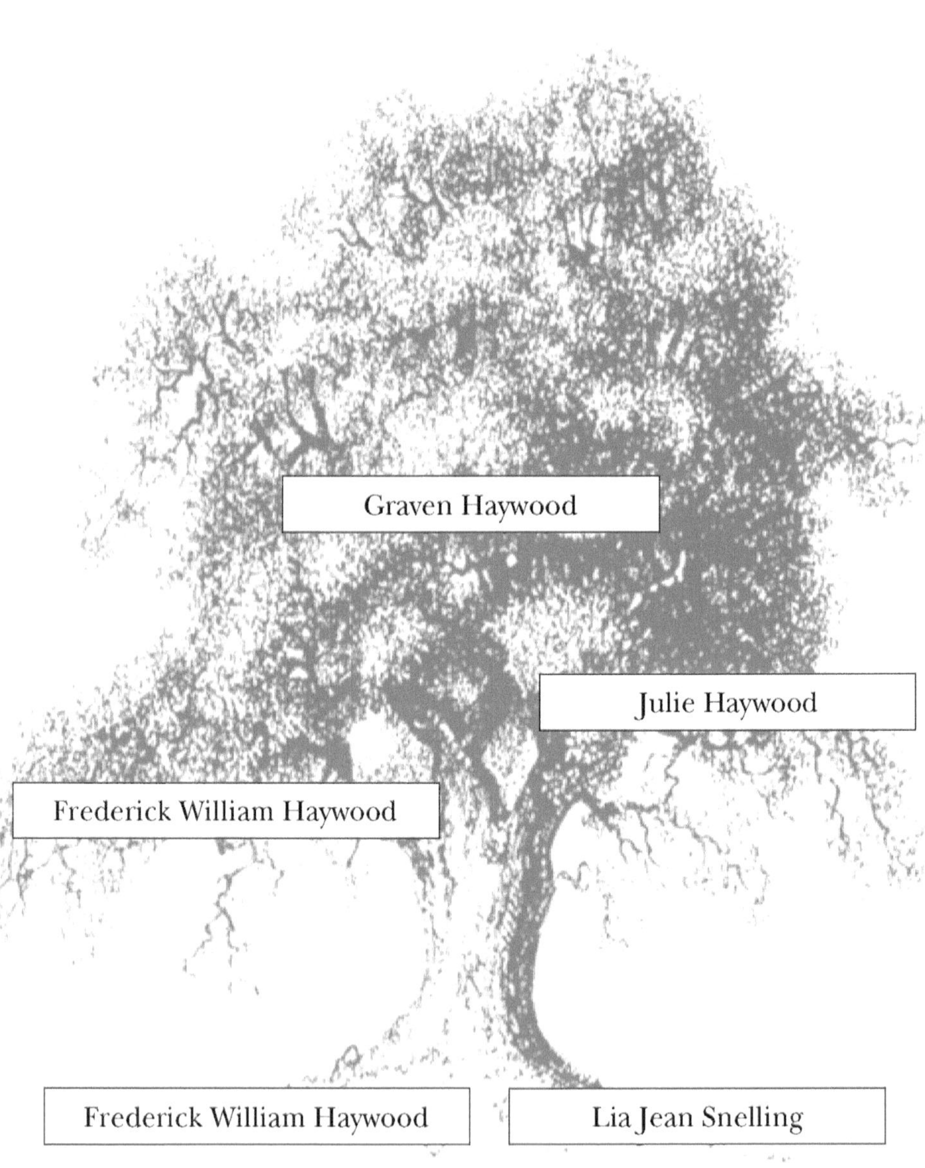

HAYWOOD-WILLER

HAYWOOD

HULLEY-BECHARD

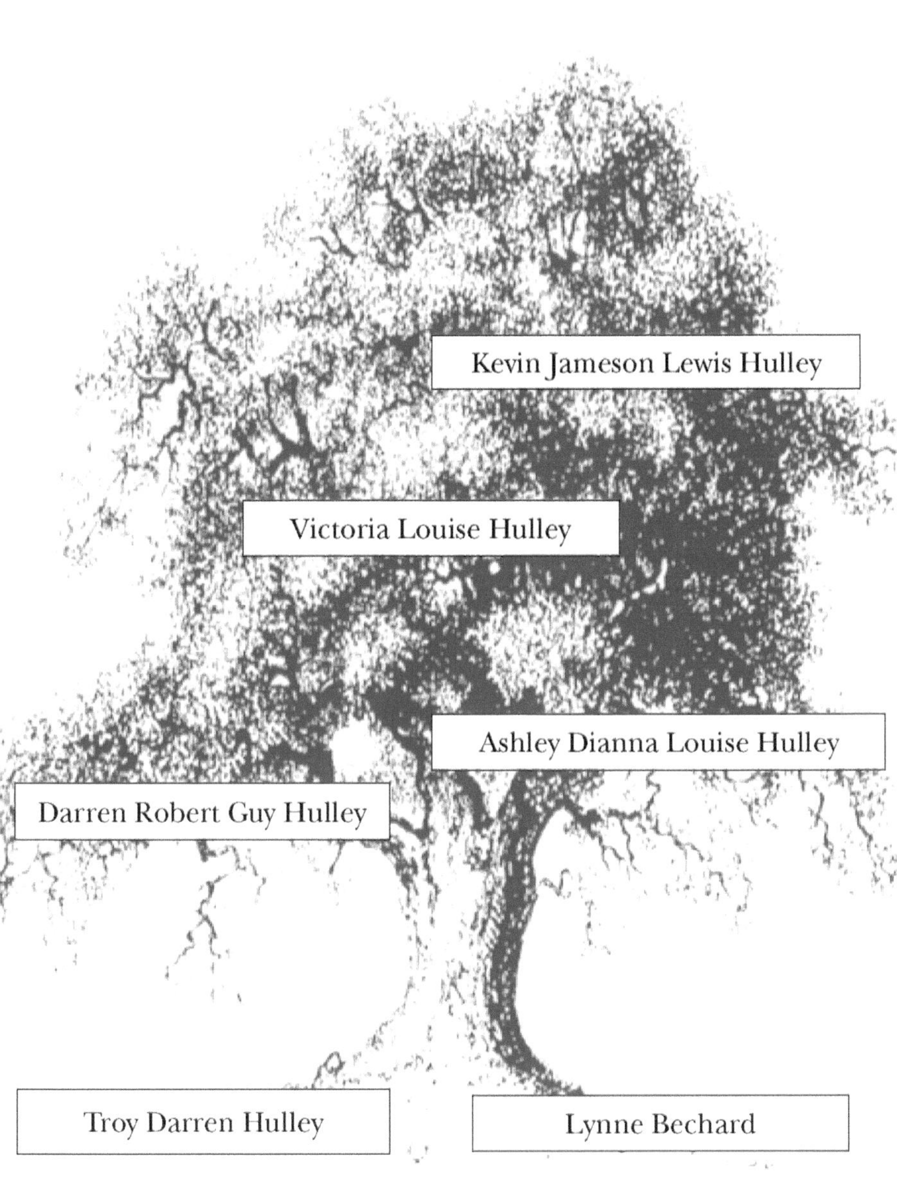

HULLEY-GURNEY

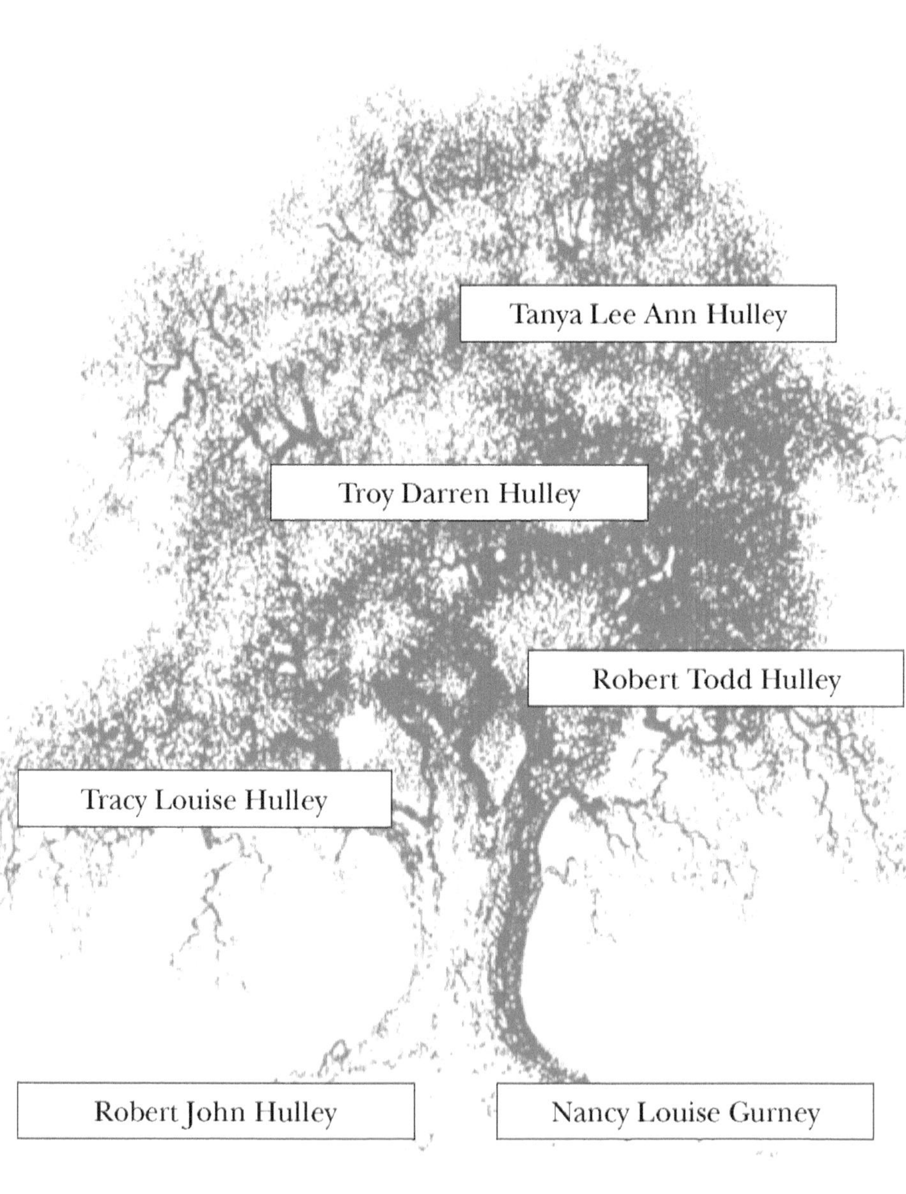

HULLEY-MARYVILLE

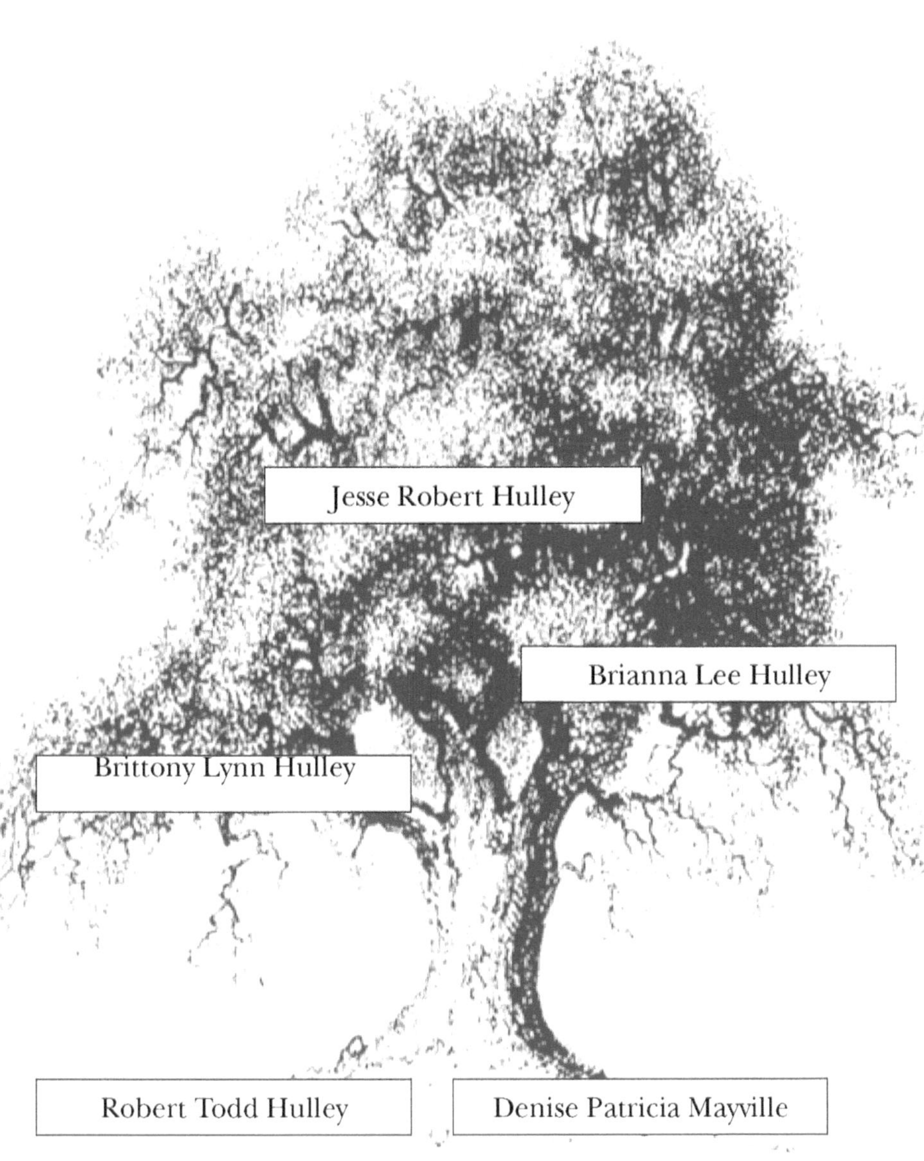

HUXLEY-HULLEY

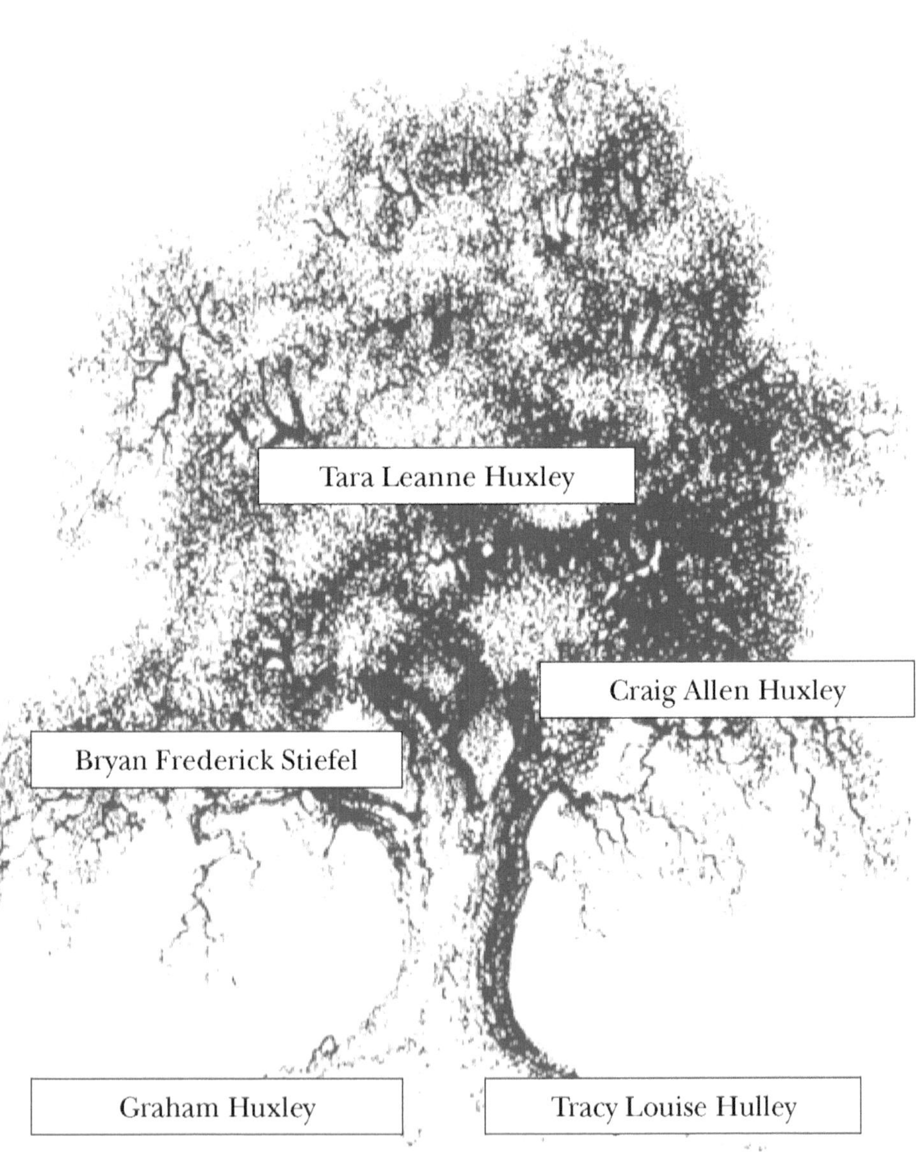

JOHNSON-HAYWOOD

KINSMAN-GURNEY

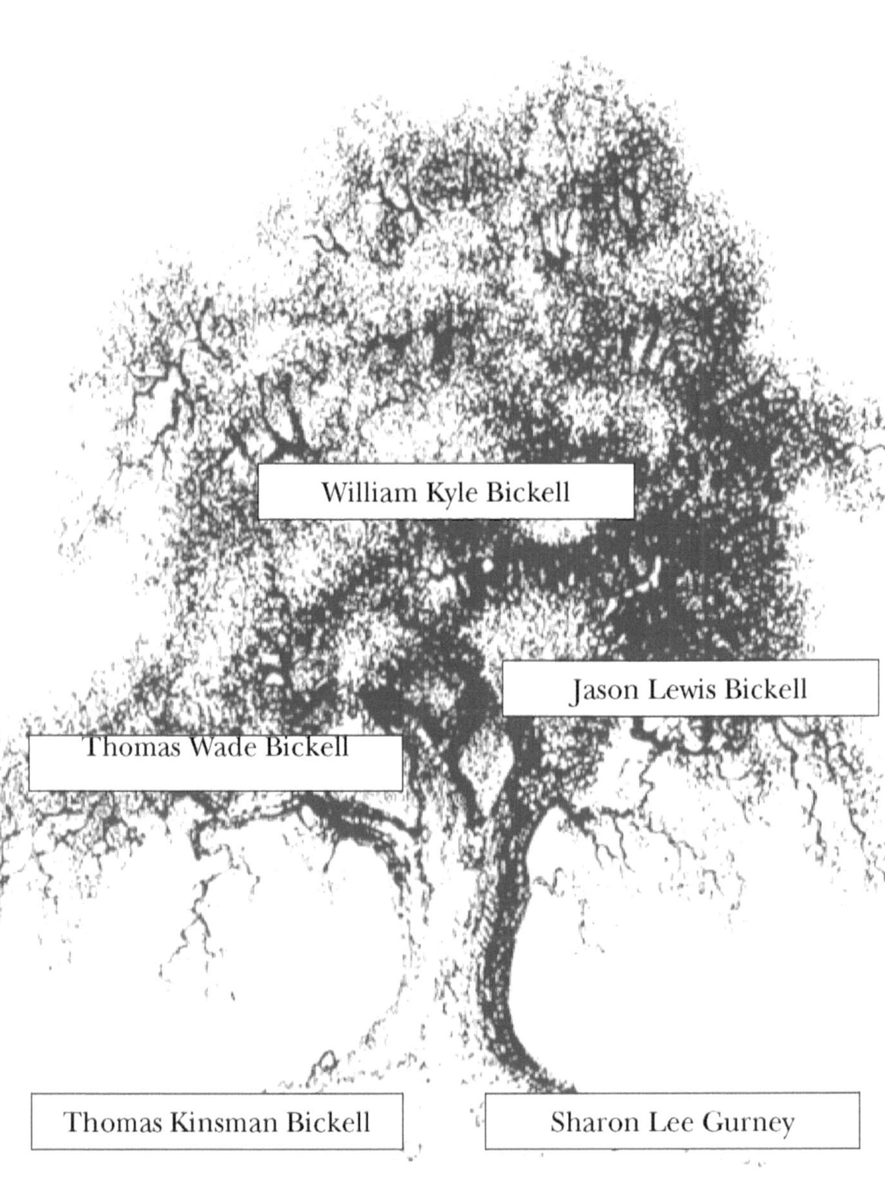

KNOX-GRAHAM

Max Peter Knox
Ellie Grace Knox
Peter Martin Knox
Kim Graham

NORRIS-ALLEN

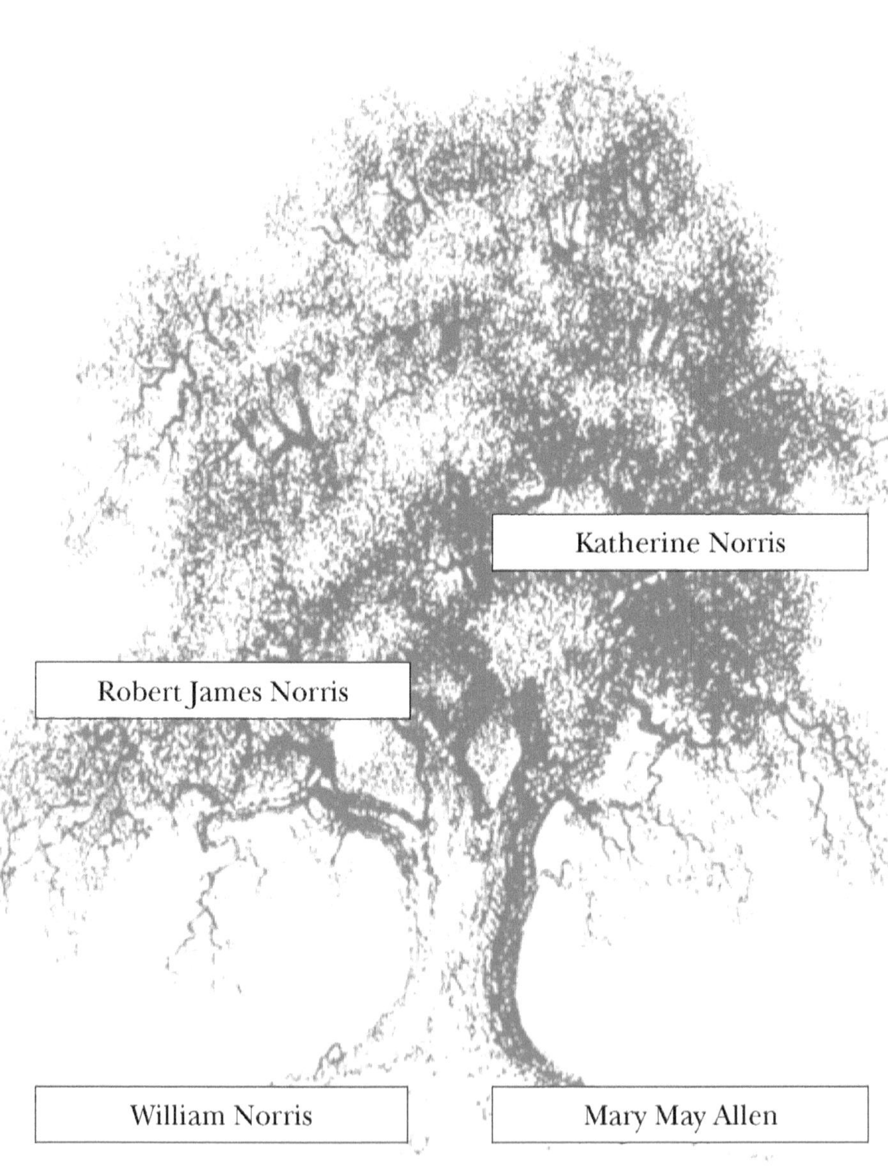

PETERS-HAYWOOD

ROBERTS-HAYES

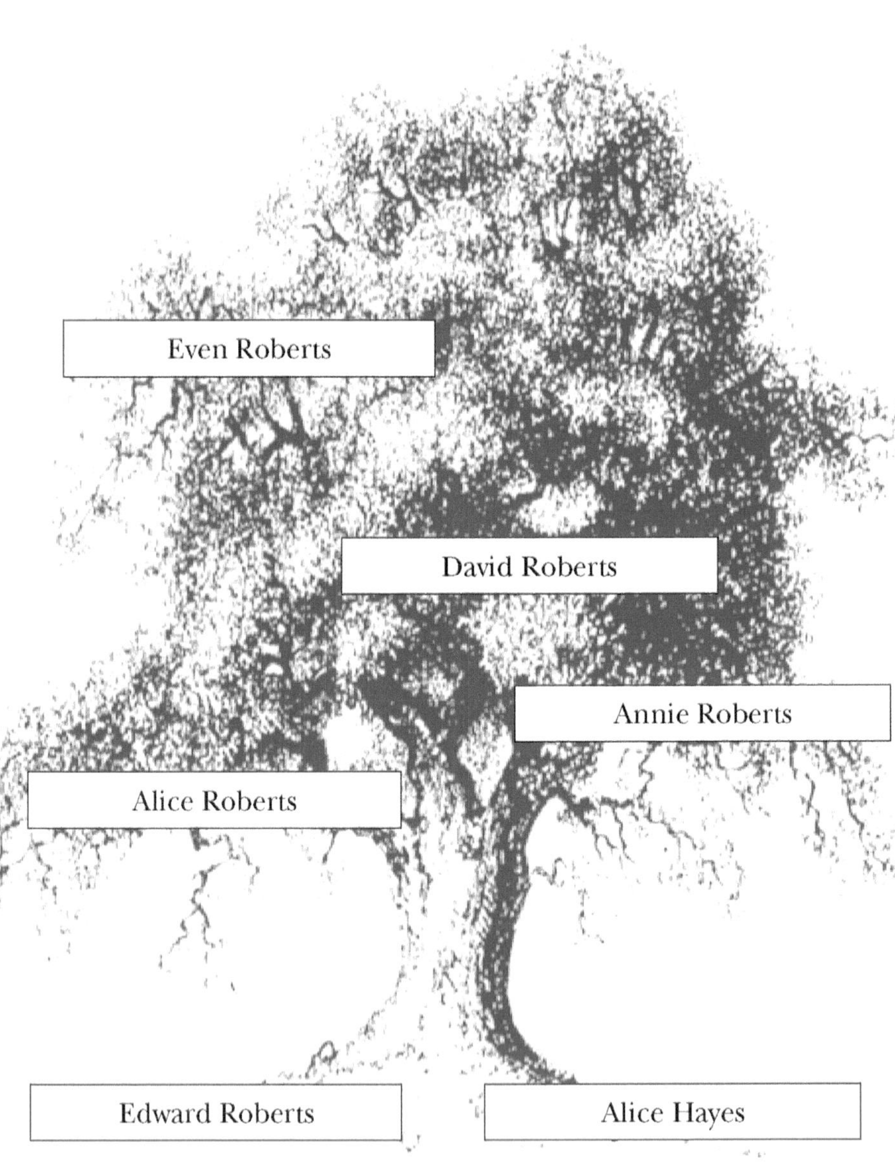

SCEA-SIMPSON

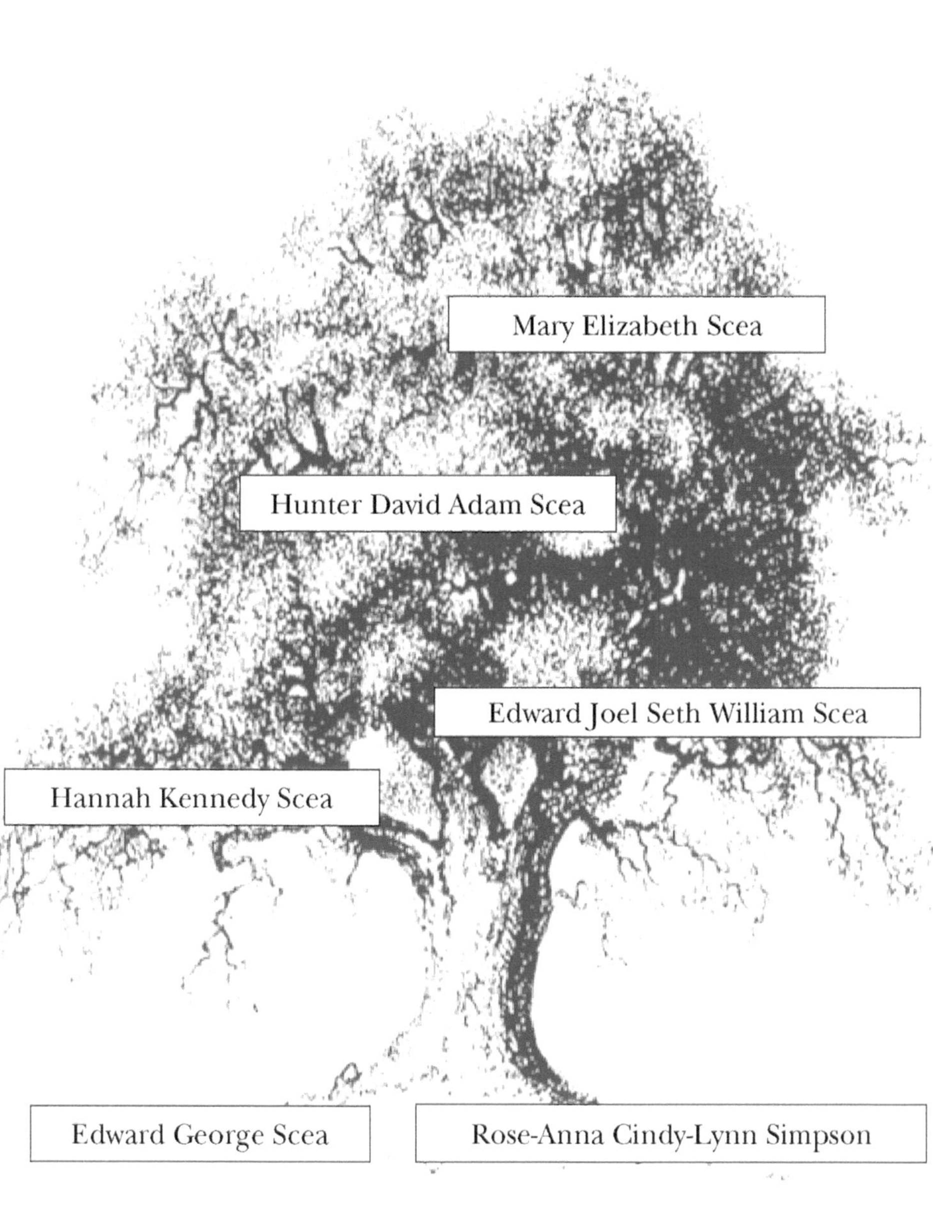

SHERRATT-GURNEY

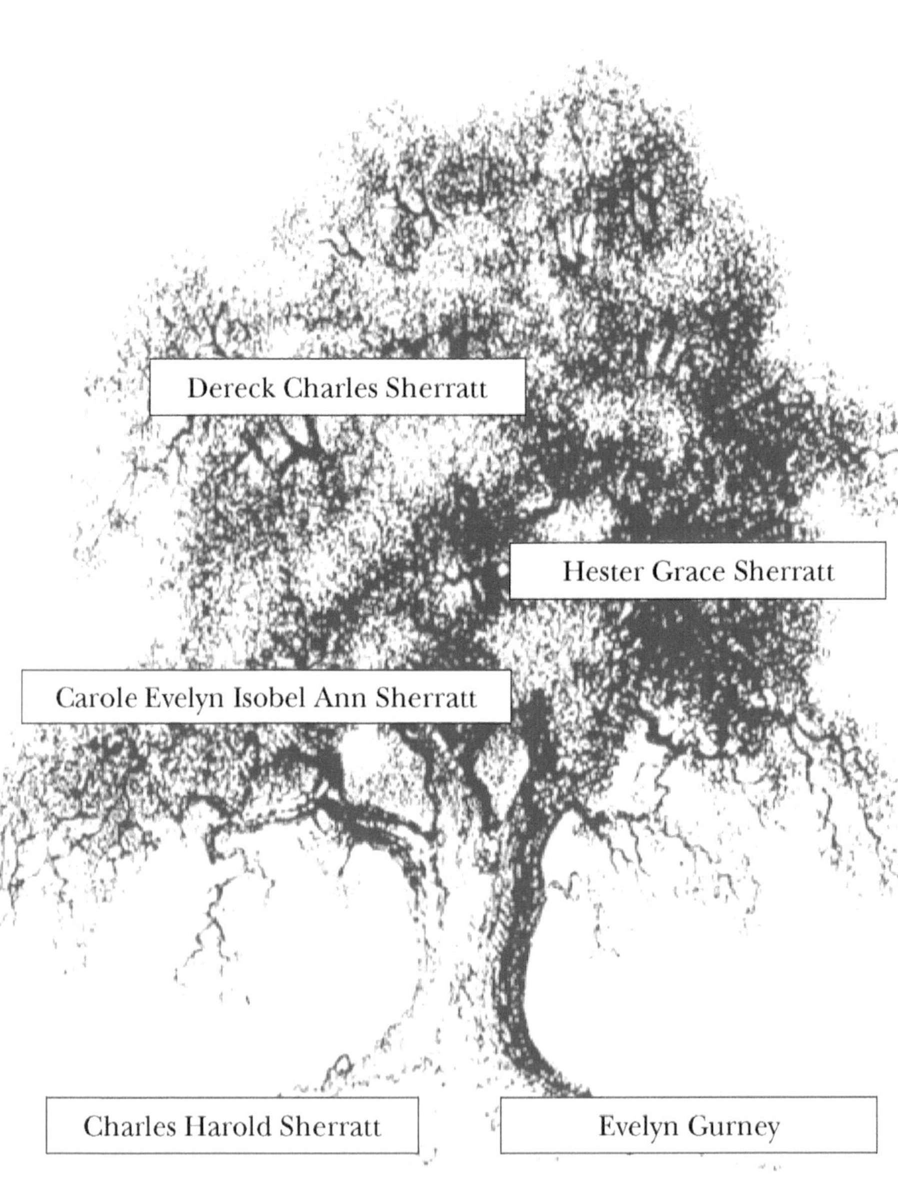

SHERRATT-WORKMAN

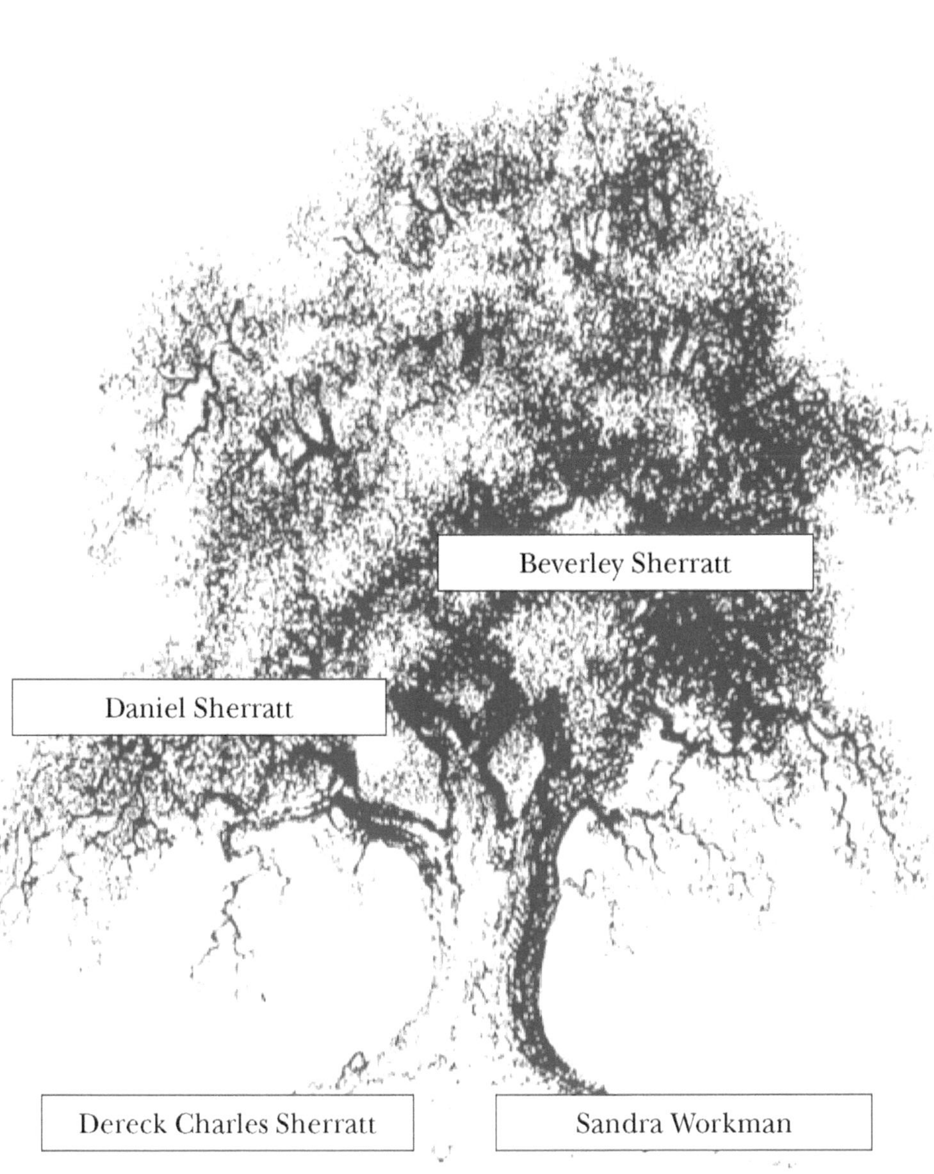

SIMPSON-ANDERSON

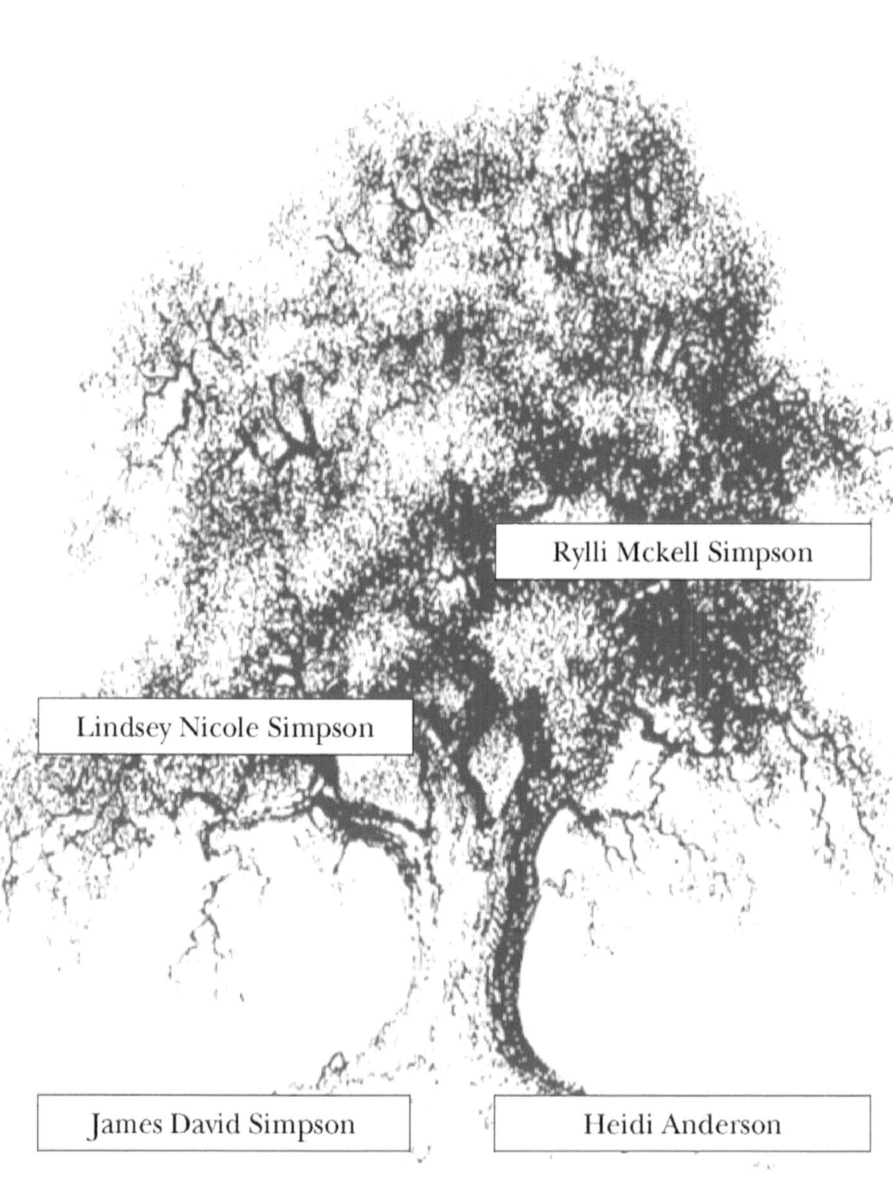

SIMPSON-CAMPBELL

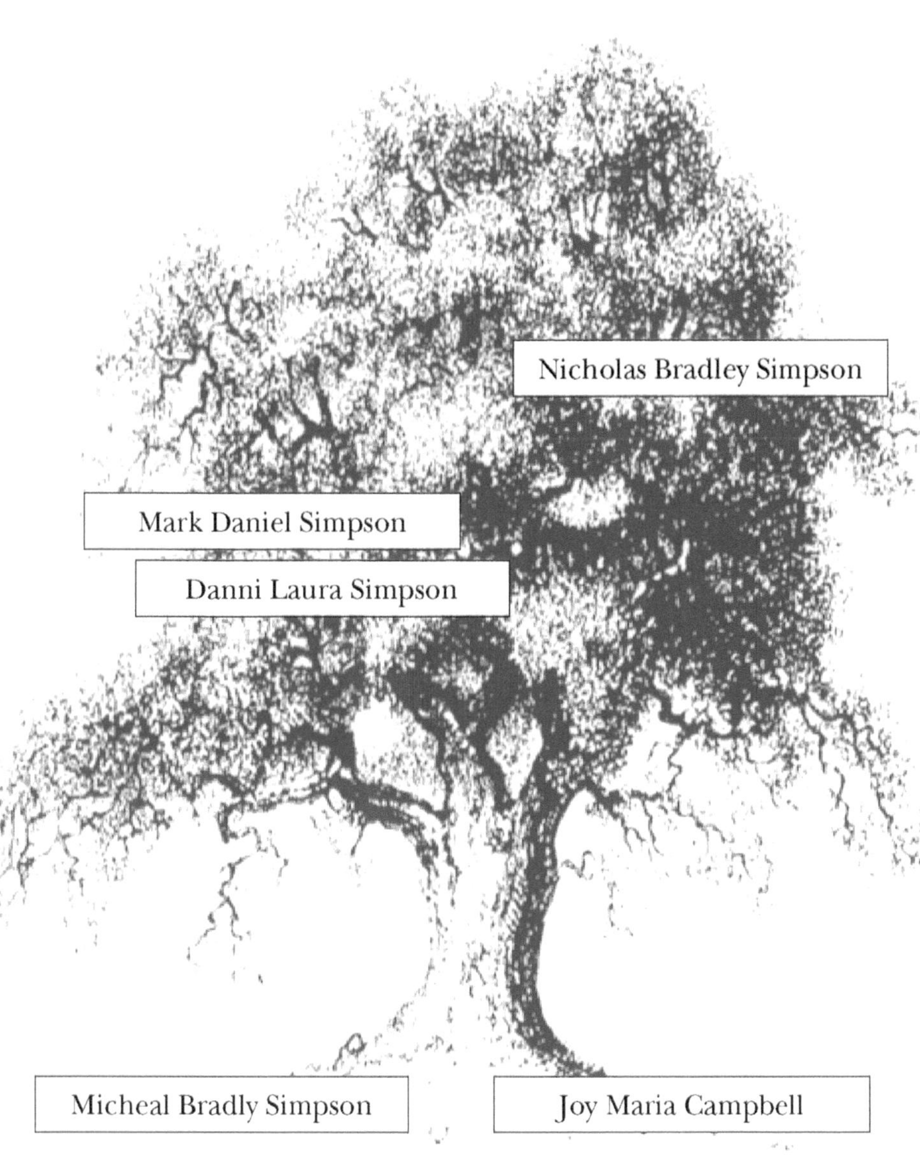

SIMPSON-HAYWOOD

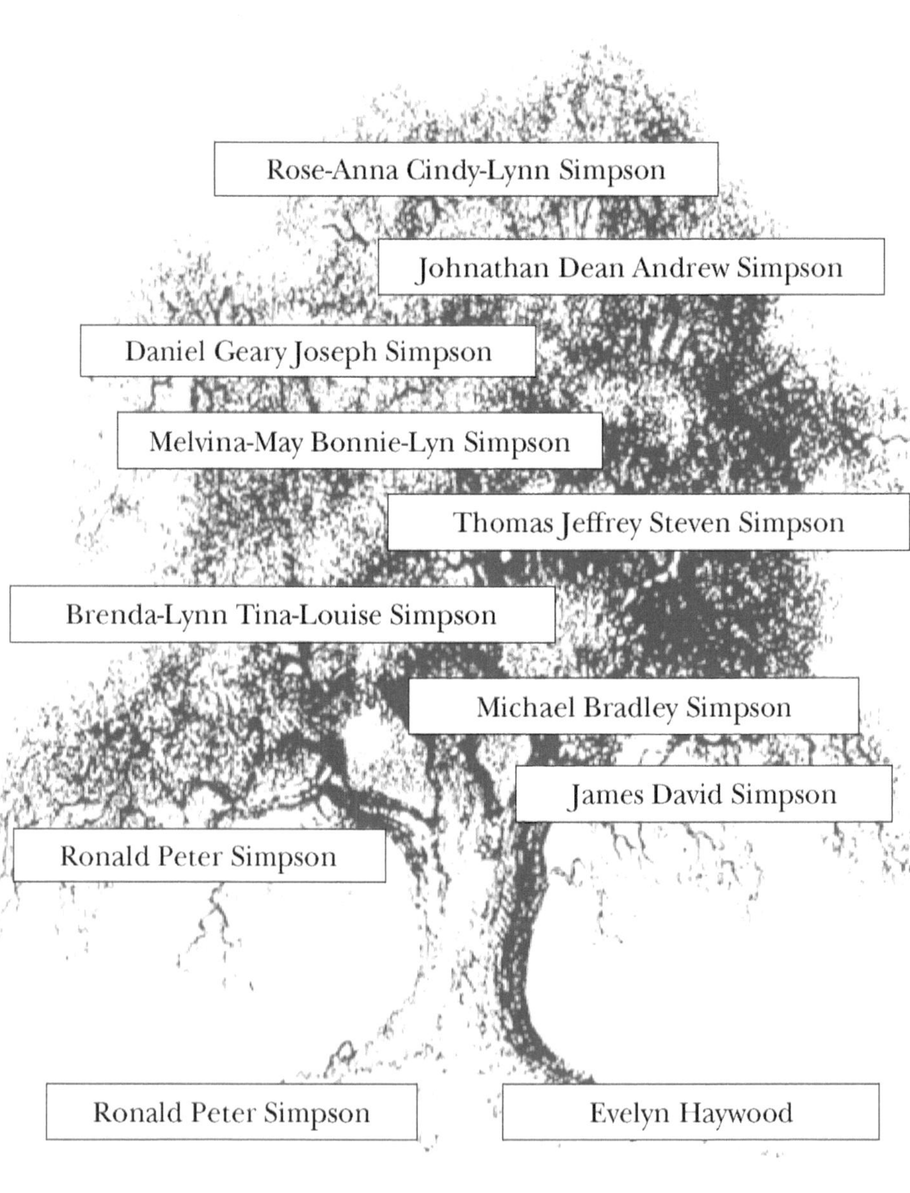

SIMPSON-SULMONA

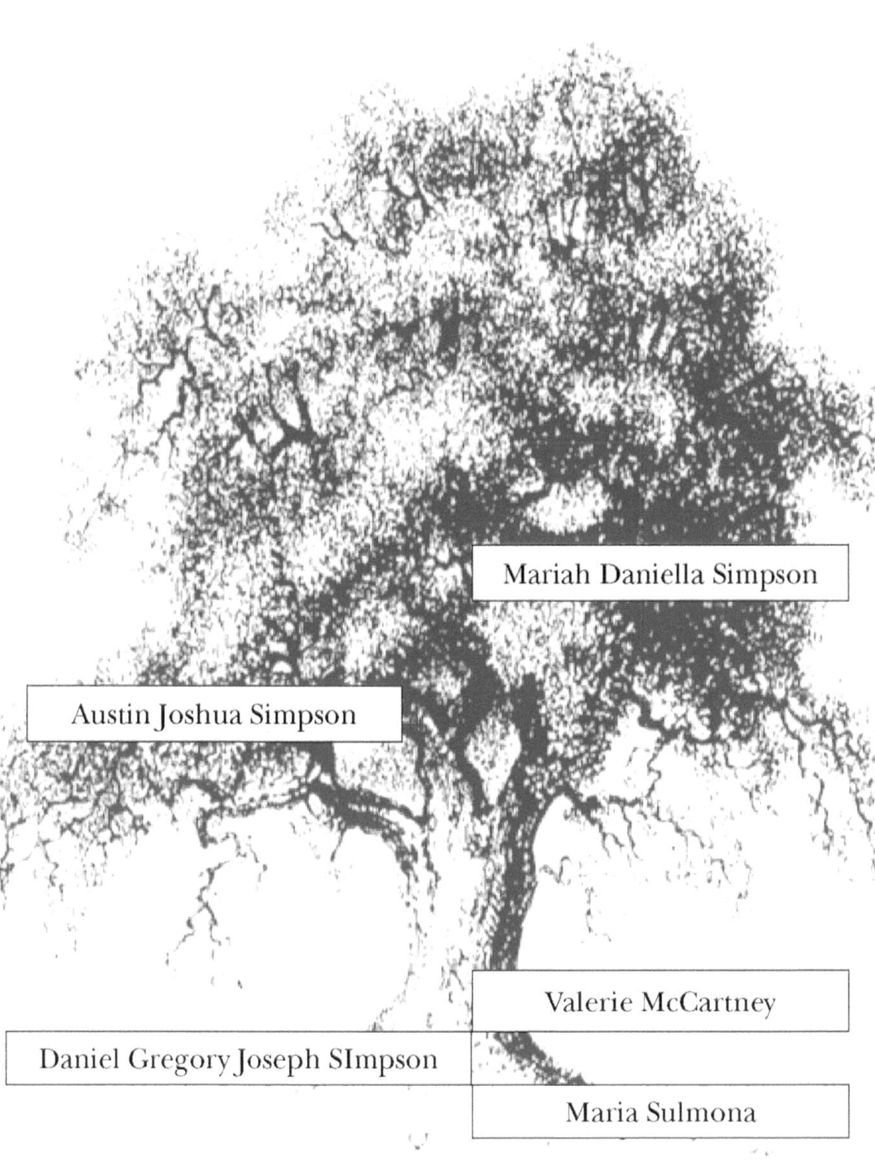

SQUIRE-GURNEY

SQUIRE-HARRISON

SQUIRE-LEMON

SQUIRE-MOYER

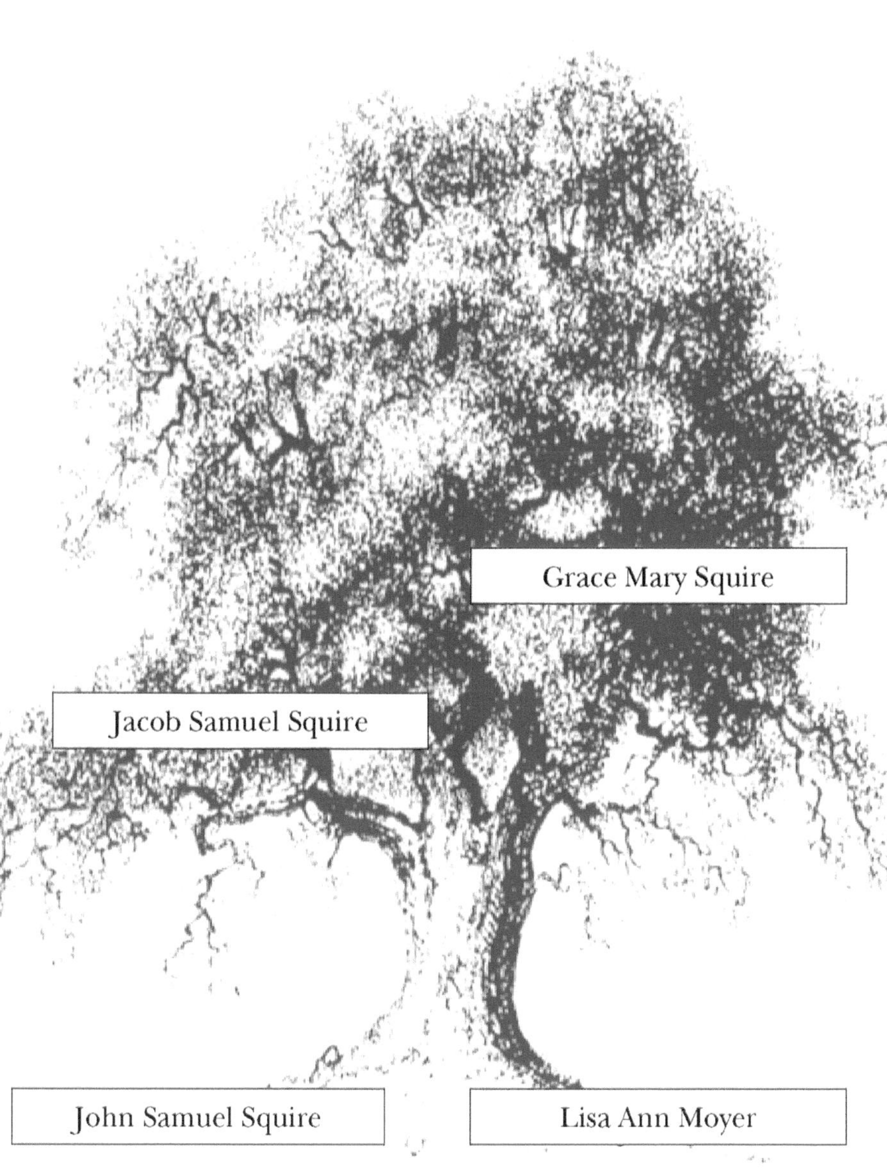

STIEFEL-MCLAREN

TURKEY-HAYWOOD

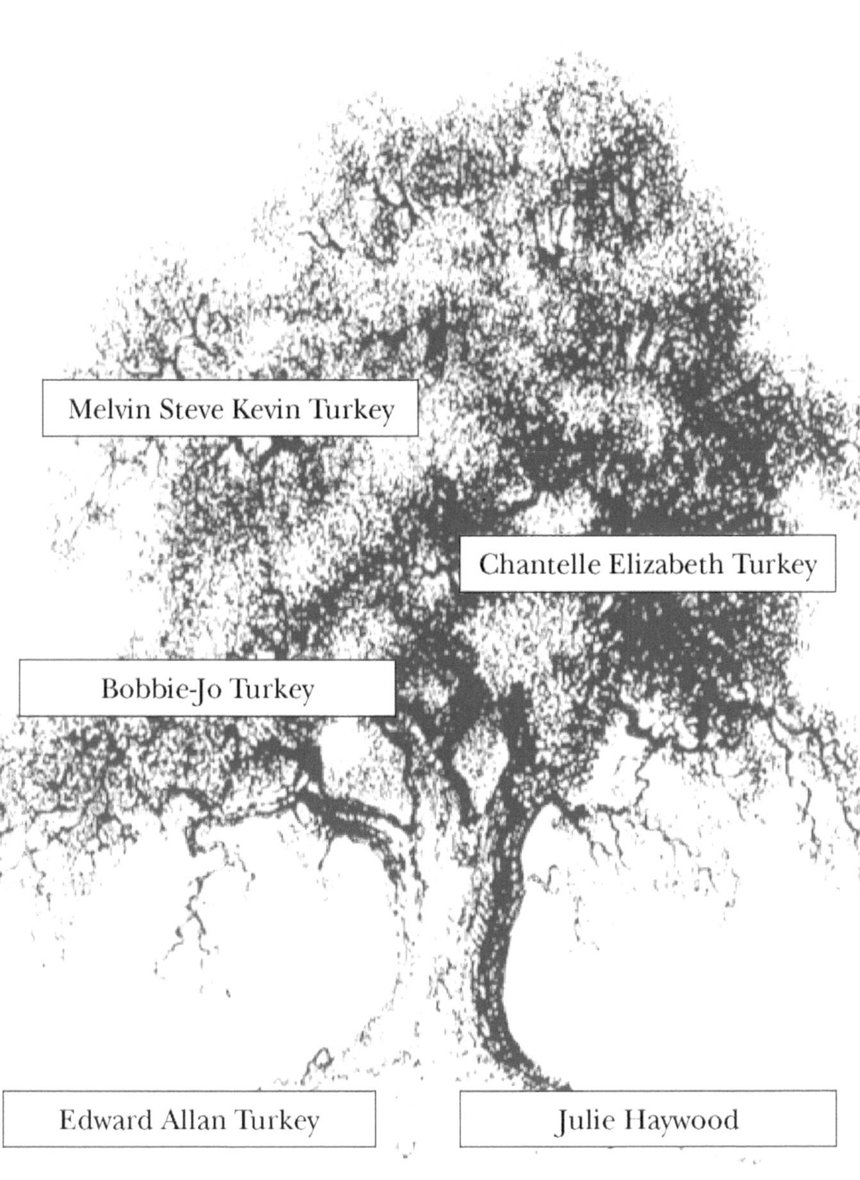

VAN DYK-HULLEY

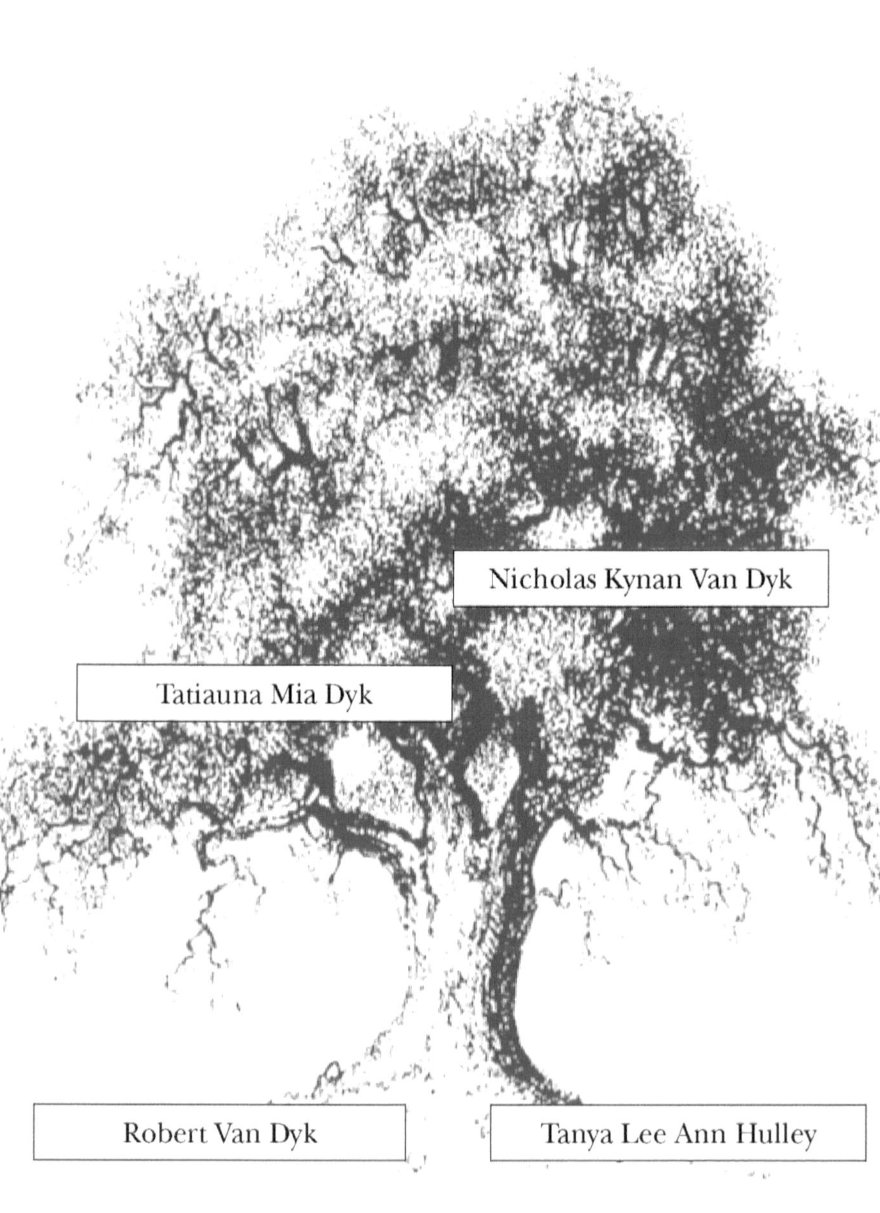

WALLACE-CARR

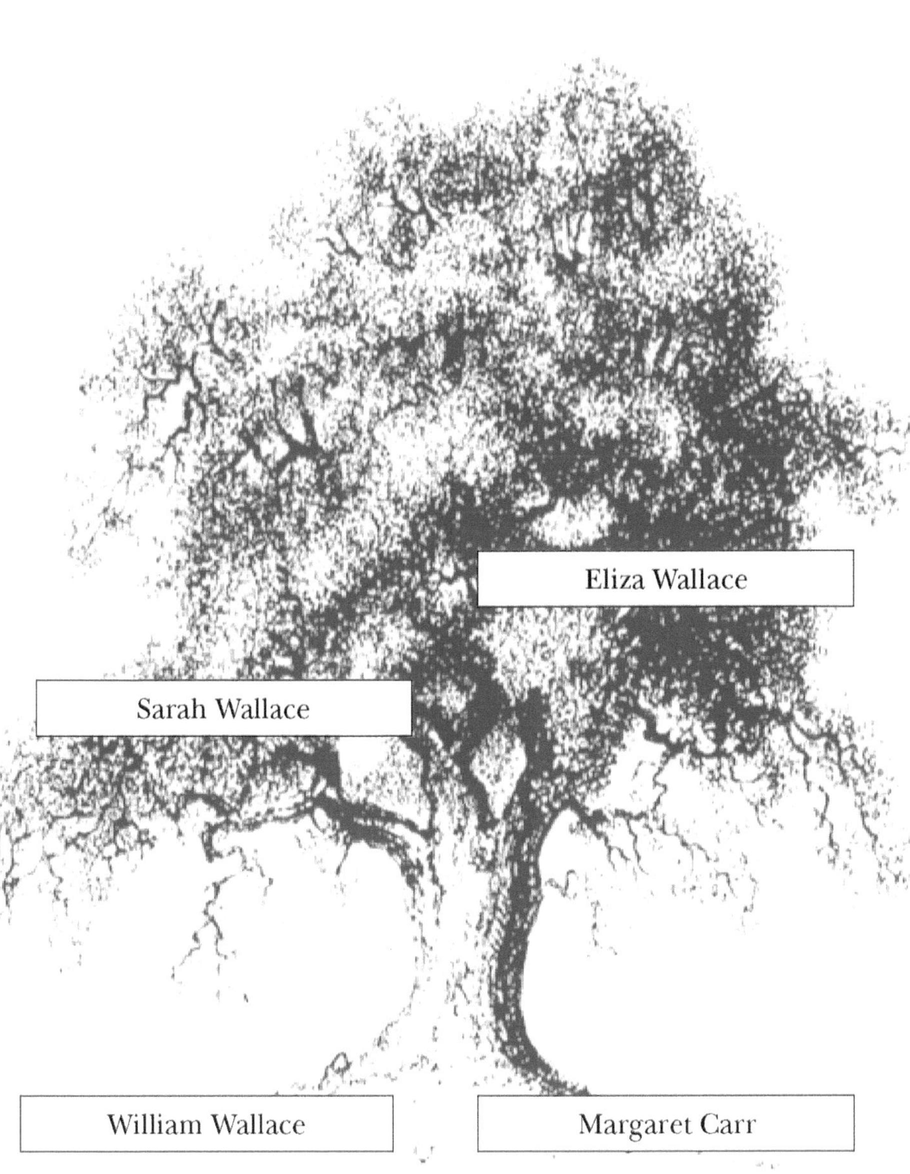

WHITE-SIMPSON

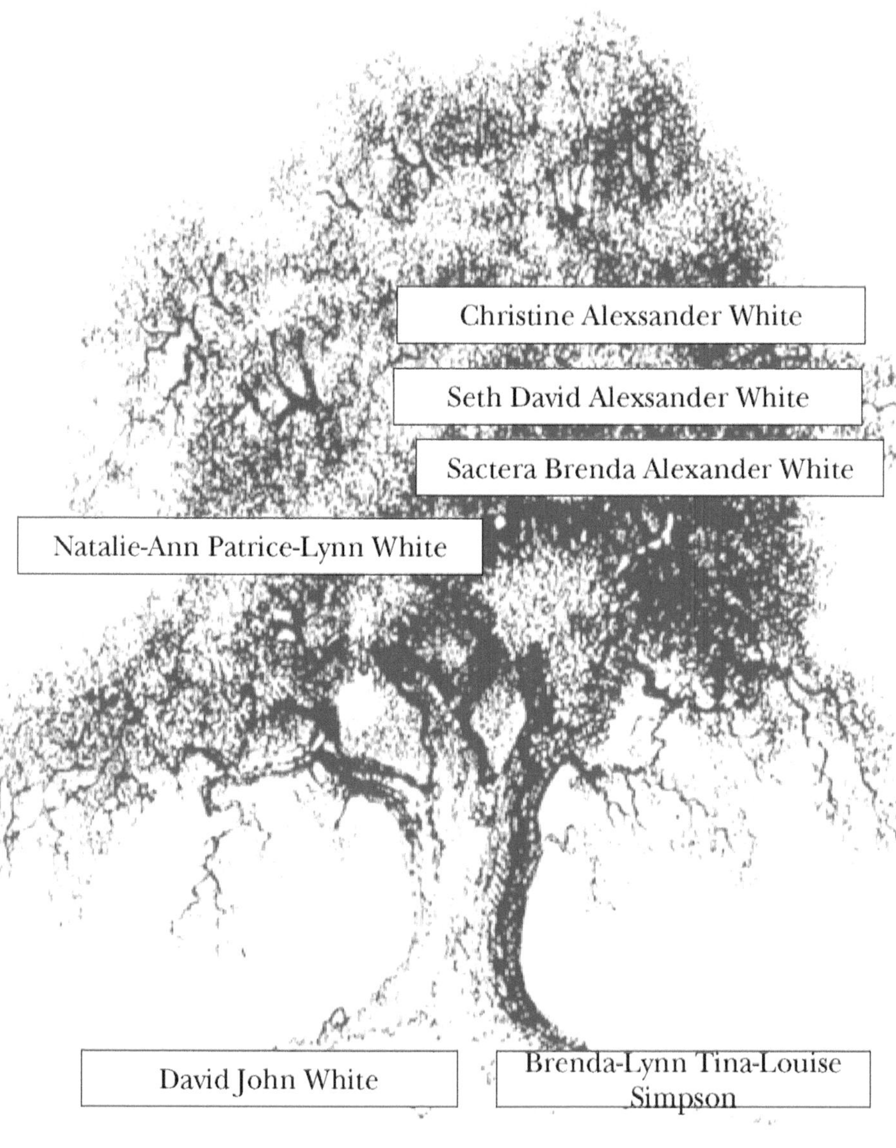

CERTIFICATES

Canadian Passenger Lists, 1865-1935

Mary

Name:	**Minnie Gurney**
Gender:	**Female**
Age:	**21**
Estimated birth year:	**abt 1909**
Birth Country:	**Northern Ireland**
Date of Arrival:	**2 May 1930**
Vessel:	**Duchess of Bedford**
Search Ship Database:	View the 'Duchess of Bedford' in the 'Passenger Ships and Images' database
Port of Arrival:	**Montreal, Quebec**
Port of Departure:	**Belfast, Northern Ireland**
Roll:	**T-14762**

Source Information:
Ancestry.com. *Canadian Passenger Lists, 1865-1935* [database on-line]. Provo, UT, USA: The Generations Network, Inc., 2008. Original data: Library and Archives Canada. *Passenger Lists, 1865-1935*. Ottawa, Canada: Library and Archives Canada. RG76, T-479 to T-520, T-4689 to T-4874, T-14700 to T-14939, C-4511 to C-4542.

Description:
This database contains passenger lists of ships arriving in various Canadian ports, as well as a few eastern U.S. ports, from 1865-1935. Information listed in these records includes: name of passenger, age, gender, marital status, birth country, nationality, occupation, and religious affiliation. [illegible]

Deimhniú Breithe | **Birth Certificate**

Arna h-eisiúint de bhun an Achta um Chlárú Sibhialta 2004 | Issued in pursuance of the Civil Registration Act 2004

Éire | **Ireland**

Uimhir Chláraithe / Registration Number: 1188866

Breith a Chláraíodh i gCeantar / Birth Registered in the district of: Londonderry Urban 2

I gCeantar an Chláraitheora Maoirseachta / In the Superintendent Registrar's District of: Derry

I gContae / In the County of: Co. Derry

Dáta Breithe / Date of Birth; Ionad Breithe / Place of Birth	Ainm / Name	Gnéas / Sex	Ainm, Sloinne agus Ionad Chónaithe an Athar / Name and Surname and Dwelling-Place of Father	Ainm agus Sloinne na Máthar agus a sloinne roimh phósadh di / Name and Surname and Maiden name of Mother	Céim nó Gairm Bheatha an Athar / Rank or Profession of Father	Síniú, Cáilíocht agus Ionad Chónaithe an Fhaisnéiseora / Signature, Qualification and Residence of Informant	An Dáta a Cláraíodh / When Registered	Síniú an Chláraitheora / Signature of Registrar	Ainm Baiste má tugadh é tar éis chlárú na Breithe agus an Dáta / Baptismal Name if added after Registration of Birth and Date
[illegible] 21 third [illegible] Lewis St	Evelyn	F	William Gurney 3 Lewis St	Sarah Gurney formerly Wallace	Baker	Sarah [illegible] Campbell Present at birth [illegible] Wesley St	Seventh July 1921	[illegible] Foster Registrar	

Arna dheimhniú mar shliocht cruinn ... / Certified to be compiled from a register maintained under section 13 of the Civil Registration Act 2004

Eisithe ag / Issued by **Michelle Wallace, GRO** Dáta / Date Of Issue 31 July 2008

Is cion trom é an deimhniú seo a athrú nó é a úsáid tar éis a athraithe / To alter this certificate or to use it as altered is a serious offence

Deimhniú Breithe | **Birth Certificate**

Arna h-eisiúint de bhun an Achta um Chlárú Sibhialta 2004 | Issued in pursuance of the Civil Registration Act 2004

Éire | **Ireland**

Uimhir Chláraithe / Registration Number: 1184629

Breith a Chláraíodh i gCeantar / Birth Registered in the district of: Londonderry Urban 2

I gCeantar an Chláraitheora Maoirseachta / In the Superintendent Registrar's District of: Derry

I gContae / In the County of: Co. Derry

Dáta Breithe / Date of Birth; Ionad Breithe / Place of Birth	Ainm / Name	Gnéas / Sex	Ainm, Sloinne agus Ionad Chónaithe an Athar / Name and Surname and Dwelling-Place of Father	Ainm agus Sloinne na Máthar agus a sloinne roimh phósadh di / Name and Surname and Maiden name of Mother	Céim nó Gairm Bheatha an Athar / Rank or Profession of Father	Síniú, Cáilíocht agus Ionad Chónaithe an Fhaisnéiseora / Signature, Qualification and Residence of Informant	An Dáta a Cláraíodh / When Registered	Síniú an Chláraitheora / Signature of Registrar	Ainm Baiste má tugadh é tar éis chlárú na Breithe agus an Dáta / Baptismal Name if added after Registration of Birth and Date
1914 fifteenth June Lewis St	Lewis	M	William Gurney 3 Lewis St	Sarah Gurney formerly Wallace	Baker	William Gurney Father 3 Lewis St	Fourteenth August 1914	[illegible] Foster Registrar	

Arna dheimhniú mar shliocht cruinn ... / Certified to be compiled from a register maintained under section 13 of the Civil Registration Act 2004

Eisithe ag / Issued by **Michelle Wallace, GRO** Dáta / Date Of Issue 31 July 2008

Is cion trom é an deimhniú seo a athrú nó é a úsáid tar éis a athraithe / To alter this certificate or to use it as altered is a serious offence

The Births and Deaths Registration (Northern Ireland) Order 1976, Article 34

CERTIFIED  COPY

Ref: 051393/07

DEATH Registered in the district of LONDONDERRY

D80/X1/OR60

1	Name & surname	Margaret Allen
2	Sex	Female
3	Date of death	Seventeenth December 1980
4	Place of death	75a Heron Way, Clooney Estate, Londonderry
5	Usual address (if different from place of death)	———
6	Marital status	Married
7	Date & place of birth	10 September 1905 Londonderry
8	Occupation	Wife of Robert Allen, a retired general labourer
9	Maiden surname (of woman who has married)	Gurney
10	Cause of death	I a Coronary thrombosis b Arthritis of hip Certified
11	Qualification of informant	Son
12	Address of informant	58 Emerson Street, Waterside, Londonderry
13	Signature of informant	William L Allen
14	Date of registration	22 December 1980
15	Signature of Registrar	Deputy Registrar

CERTIFIED to be a true copy of an entry in a register in the custody of the Registrar General and given under the SEAL of the General Register Office, Belfast.

this 26th day of August 2008

The Registrar General shall cause any certified copy of an entry given in the General Register Office to be stamped with the seal of the Office of which judicial notice shall be taken

[illegible] OF MARRIAGE	PLACE	LICENCE OR BANNS
September 22nd 1934.	St Tim[illegible]'s.	Banns.

[illegible] GROOM	RELIGIOUS DENOMINATION	BRIDE	RELIGIOUS DENOMINATION
Frederick William Haywood	Ch of E.	Minnie Gurney	Church of England

BACHELOR OR WIDOWER	SPINSTER OR WIDOW
B.	S.

OCCUPATION	PLACE OF BIRTH	OCCUPATION	PLACE OF BIRTH
Night Stripper	Sorrel - Quebec	Domestic Servant	Londonderry Ireland.

AGE	RESIDENCE	AGE	RESIDENCE
26.	698 Ontario Street	24.	23 Glen Elm Terr

[illegible] FULL NAME AND OCCUPATION: Frederick William Haywood - Salesman.

FATHER'S FULL NAME AND OCCUPATION: William Gurney. Baker.

[illegible] NAME: Annie Robbins.

MOTHER'S MAIDEN NAME: Sarah Wallace

[illegible] OF GROOM: [illegible]rederick William Haywood

SIGNATURE OF BRIDE: Minnie Gurney

SIGNATURES OF WITNESSES

[illegible]: Doris Gwendolyn Haywood

[illegible]: 698 Ontario Street

[illegible]: Harry Gee

[illegible]: 84 Humber Blvd

NAME

ADDRESS

NAME

ADDRESS

Signature and Address of Clergyman

REGISTRATION OF BIRTHS AND DEATHS IN NORTHERN IRELAND.

CERTIFIED COPY OF ENTRY IN THE REGISTER OF BIRTHS

Pursuant to 43 & 44 Vic., Cap. 13.

[illegible] Registered in the District of L. Derry Urban No. 2 in the Superintendent Registrar's District of Derry in the County of [illegible]

Date and Place of Birth (1)	Name (if any) (2)	Sex (3)	Name and Surname and Dwelling place of Father (4)	Name and Surname and Maiden Surname of Mother (5)	Rank or Profession of Father (6)	Signature, Qualification and Residence of Informant (7)	When Registered (8)	Signature of Registrar (9)
1908 Thirty first May 77 Creggan Rd	Mary	F	William Gurney 77 Creggan Rd.	Sarah Gurney formerly Wallace	Baker	Kathleen her O'Connell mark Present at birth 20 Creggan Rd	Sixteenth June 1908	T. [illegible] Asst Registrar

I hereby Certify that the above is a true Copy of an Entry in a Register of Births in my custody.

Office, Londonderry

Date, 25th June, 1951

[illegible] Registrar

CAUTION.—Any person who (1) falsifies any of the particulars on this Certificate, or (2) uses a falsified Certificate as true, knowing it to be false, is liable to prosecution under the Forgery Act, 1913.

REGISTRATION OF MARRIAGE IN NORTHERN IRELAND

Certified copy of an Entry in Marriage Registration Records

Marriage (Northern Ireland) Order 2003

Registrar's District of

solemnized at [illegible] in the [illegible] of [illegible] in the [illegible]

Name and Surname	Age	Condition	Rank or Profession	Residence at the Time of Marriage	Father's Name and Surname	Rank or Profession of Father
Robert [illegible]	31	Bachelor	Labourer	[illegible] Road	Robert [illegible]	[illegible]
Margaret [illegible]	[illegible]	Spinster	[illegible]	3 [illegible] Road Londonderry	William [illegible]	Baker

[illegible] according to the Rites and Ceremonies of the Church of Ireland [illegible] by me [illegible]

Robert [illegible] | in the Presence of us, | [illegible]

Margaret [illegible] | | [illegible]

Certified to be a true copy of an entry in the Marriage Registration Records in the custody of the Registrar General for Northern Ireland and given under the Seal of the General Register Office on 20th August 2008

The Registrar General shall cause any certified copy of an entry given in the General Register Office to be stamped with the seal of the Office of which judicial notice shall be taken.

Brook Street Avenue, Derry

CENSUS OF IRELAND, 1901.

FORM A.

No. on Form B. [illegible]

[illegible] of the MEMBERS of this FAMILY and their VISITORS, BOARDERS, SERVANTS, &c., who slept or abode in this House on the night of SUNDAY, the 31st of MARCH, 1901.

Christian Name	Surname	Relation to Head of Family	Religious Profession	Education	Age	Sex	Rank, Profession, or Occupation	Marriage	Where Born	Irish Language	If Deaf and Dumb; Dumb only; Blind; Imbecile or Idiot; or Lunatic
[illegible]	[illegible]	Head	Church of Ireland	Read & Write	[illegible]	M	Baker	Married	Londonderry		
[illegible]	[illegible]	Wife	Church of Ireland	Read & Write	21	F		Married	Londonderry		

I hereby certify, as required by the Act 63 Vic., cap. 6, s. 6 (1), that the foregoing Return is correct, according to the best of my knowledge and belief.

[illegible] (Signature of Enumerator.)

I believe the foregoing to be a true Return.

William [illegible] (Signature of Head of Family.)

PROOF OF DEATH CERTIFICATE

DECEASED

Friend
Last Name at Time of Death

William John
Given Name(s)

January 5, 1937
Date of Birth

June 20, 2012
Date of Death

PLACE OF DEATH

Toronto
City/Town

Ontario, Canada
Province/Country

Given under my hand at Toronto in the Province of Ontario, June 21, 2012

Certified as per our records

Turner & Porter

Funeral Directors Limited

Per [signature]

2357 Bloor Street West, Toronto, Ontario, M6S 1P4

PICTURES

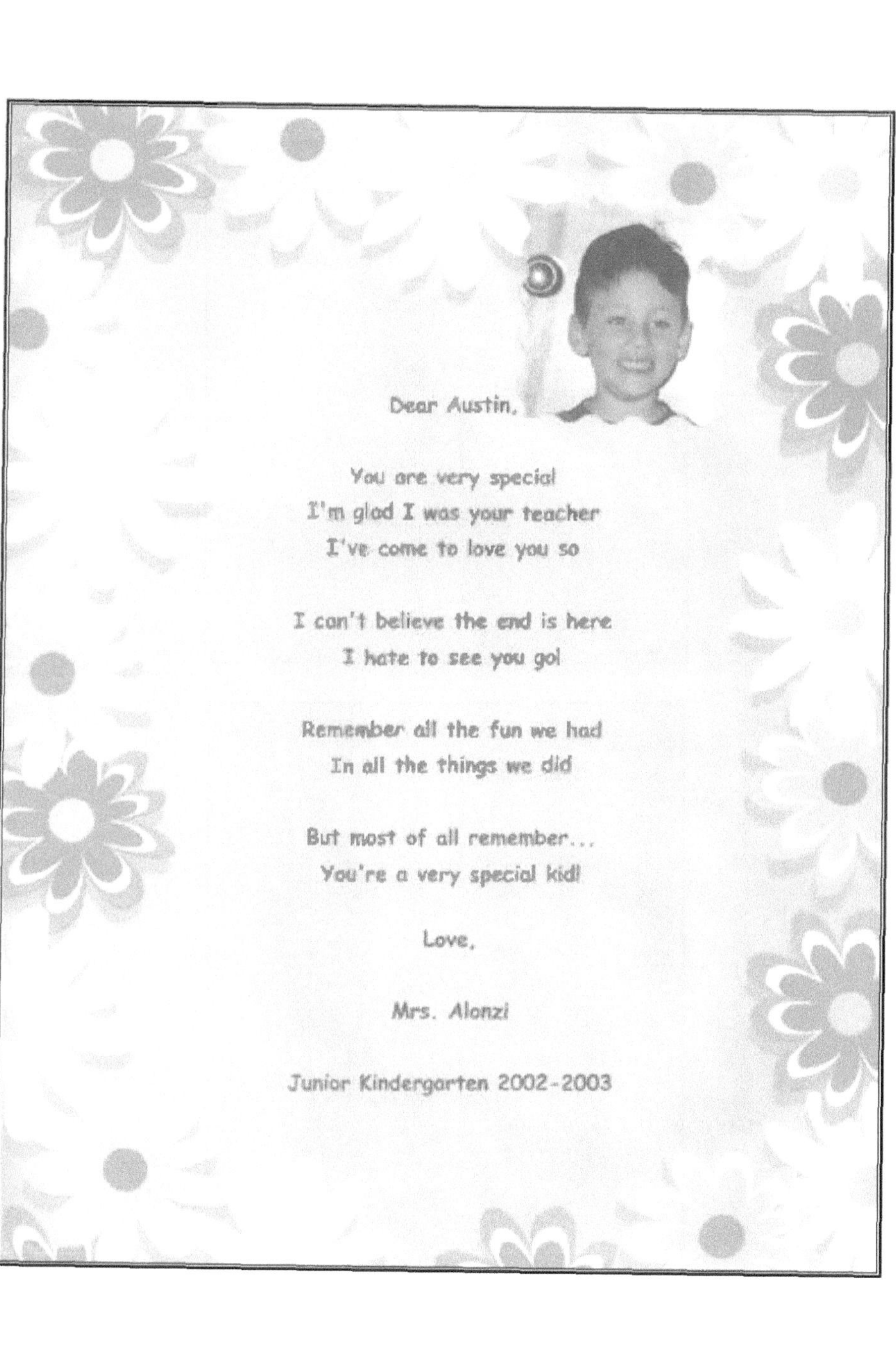

Dear Austin,

You are very special
I'm glad I was your teacher
I've come to love you so

I can't believe the end is here
I hate to see you go!

Remember all the fun we had
In all the things we did

But most of all remember...
You're a very special kid!

Love,

Mrs. Alonzi

Junior Kindergarten 2002-2003

Austin Simpson
SUPERSTAR

TREE CUTTING

Home
Find Friends

GAP

TO WED THIS MONTH

CNPS

2055

Minor Peewee Champions 2010
VISITORS
HOME

No 5. Fred & Mary's Farm

Fred and Mary's Farm, Nappanee, ON Canada

Fred Haywood at the farm

Fred and Mary at a Banquet

MONTROYAL

'06, (1906-30) 15,646. 570 x 65. Twin screw, quadruple expansion engines, 18 knots. Built by Fairfield Shipbuilding & Engineering Co. Govan, Glasgow, as **EMPRESS OF BRITAIN**; the first "Empress" on the Atlantic. M.V. Liverpool-Quebec, 5 May 1906. Collided with, and sank steamer HELVETIA in fog off Cape Magdeleine, 27 July 1912. Commissioned as armed merchant cruiser August 1914. Served as troopship 1915-19. Resumed passenger service, March 1919. Renamed MONTROYAL 1924. Broken up Stavanger, Norway 1930.

LEWIS GURNEY ARRIVED AT QUEBEC CITY
ABOARD THE MONTROYAL (ex - EMPRESS OF BRITAIN) ON AUGUST 2, 1929

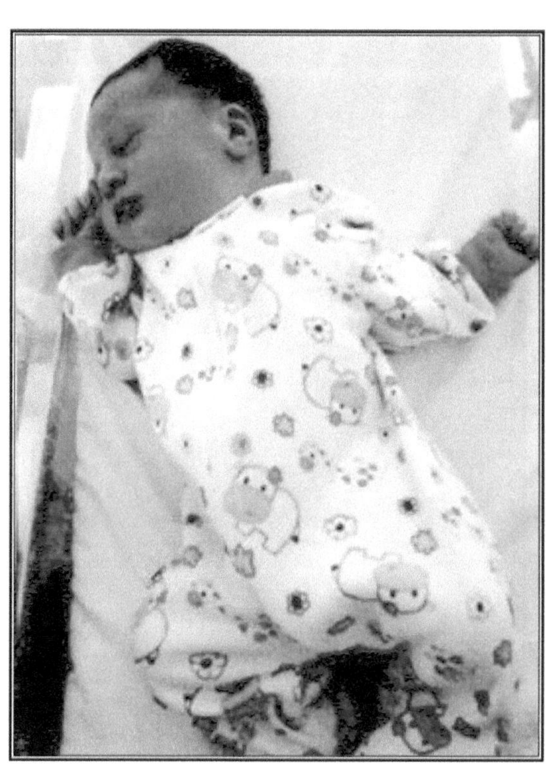

Duchess of Bedford / Empress of France (II)

The first of the four "Duchess" ships built in the late 1920's, Duchess of Bedford was built by John Brown & Co. of Glasgow. Launched by the wife of British Prime Minister Stanley Baldwin in January 1928, the ship took her maiden voyage, Liverpool-Québec-Montréal, on 24 June of the same year.

In 1933, she was chartered to Furness, Withy as a temporary running mate for the new Monarch of Bermuda. Once Queen of Bermuda was delivered to Furness, Withy, Duchess of Bedford returned to Canadian Pacific. She remained in commercial service through August 1939, served as a troopship for several months, and then returned to commercial service from January through August 1940. She then returned to trooping for the balance of the war and is credited with sinking an unidentified U-boat in August 1942.

Decommissioned in 1947, she was sent to Fairfield Shipbuilding & Engineering of Govan for refitting. Initially, she was to be renamed Empress of India, but after India gained independence, her new name was changed to Empress of France. The ship returned to service, as Empress of France, in September 1948, on her former Liverpool-Québec-Montréal route. She was given pepperpot funnels during a 1958 renovation, and remained in service until 1960, when she went to the breakers after 310 North Atlantic roundtrips.

Sister ships: Duchess of Atholl, Duchess of Richmond/Empress of Canada (III), Duchess of Cornwall/Duchess of York.

Sources: Bonsor's North Atlantic Seaway, Haws, Merchant Fleets

IT'S NOW OR NEVER
WEEK-END

B'GOSH

FAMILIES CAN BE TOGETHER FOREVER

I have a family here on earth. They are so good to me.
I want to share my life with them through all eternity.
Families can be together forever Through Heavenly Father plan.
I always want to be with my own family.
And the Lord has shown me how I can.
The Lord has shown me how I can.

While I am in my early years. I'll prepare most carefully.
So I can marry in God's temple for eternity.
Families can be together forever.
Though Heavenly Father's plan,
I always want to be with my own family.
The Lord has shown me how I can.
The Lord has shown me how I can.

NOTES

NOTES

NOTES

NOTES

NOTES

NOTES

NOTES

NOTES

NOTES

NOTES

www.ingramcontent.com/pod-product-compliance
Ingram Content Group UK Ltd.
Pitfield, Milton Keynes, MK11 3LW, UK
UKHW041855190726
13854UKWH00002B/926